D1502074

SUPREME COURT DECISIONS

Supreme Court Decisions

Scenarios, Simulations, and Activities for Understanding and Evaluating 14 Landmark Court Cases

Jeffrey D. Stocks

Prufrock Press Inc.
Waco, Texas

Edited by Jennifer Robins
Production Design by Marjorie Parker

ISBN-13: 978-1-59363-297-7
ISBN-10: 1-59363-297-5

Prufrock Press Inc.
P.O. Box 8813
Waco, TX 76714-8813
Phone: (800) 998-2208
Fax: (800) 240-0333
http://www.prufrock.com

CONTENTS

About the Book

The purpose of *Supreme Court Decisions* is to teach students about important Supreme Court cases and to help them think critically about the major historical decisions that have shaped the development of the United States. In each case presented, students will look at the issue at hand from the perspective of a person in a similar situation, make predictions, and use their knowledge of the U.S. Constitution to gain a more in-depth understanding about the case.

This book contains a list of suggested follow-up activities; a list of frequently asked questions (FAQs) and answers about the Supreme Court to provide some basic information on this institution; and 14 separate sections, each focusing on a different landmark Supreme Court case. Each section that focuses on the Supreme Court cases contains a For the Teacher insert that includes:

- an overview of the case,
- background information, and
- suggested follow-up activities.

For each case, students will receive:
- a fictional vignette or scenario,
- discussion questions,
- a recap of the actual case,
- an explanation of why the case is historically relevant.

Each section ends with a follow-up question intended to get students to think about the case's present-day relevance. The vignettes and scenarios will provide students with historical, as well as personal, perspectives of the parties involved in the case. However, please note that although these vignettes parallel actual events, the names, dialogue, letters, and in some cases, details, are purely fictional.

The cases are arranged chronologically, rather than by topic, so that students can relate each case to the historical context provided by your course. It may be worthwhile to note that the landmark cases start in the early days of the Court with rulings on broad questions regarding the role of government itself. In the 20th century, however, the landmark cases move into the realm of the individual. The last two cases studied in this book focus on the rights of individuals in schools—cases that your students should find interesting because the topics are contemporary and relevant to their own lives.

Supreme Court Decisions is intended to supplement your adopted resources and curricula that cover the landmark Supreme Court cases that have shaped America. Although this book cannot be the sole resource for such hefty topics as free speech, individual liberty, or civil rights, it does give teachers a resource designed specifically to engage students in the study of landmark cases. The author's vision of how this book could be used depends upon the nature of the course, as well as the age of the student.

An eighth-grade U.S. History class can use the early cases that fit the timeframe of the course (pre-Civil War), and any later cases that are of interest to the students or teacher. Even though the book includes some sophisticated material, the major portions are well-suited for the eighth-grade gifted student. You may find it necessary to spend more time in the actual discussion of the case studies to ensure that students understand the concepts addressed. Activities are included for enrichment purposes.

Most of the cases in *Supreme Court Decisions* fit into the timeframe of a high school U.S. History course (post-Civil War,) and all of them fit within the scope of the Advanced Placement U.S. History course. U.S. History courses can use the book at intervals throughout the year as you progress through the curriculum. Because there is not enough time in the school year to spend days discussing Supreme Court decisions, most of the activities included in the book should take no longer than one class period, with the exception of a few project-oriented activities that require students some additional time outside of class.

Finally, the book is also very suitable for a high school government class. Because the curricula of many government classes contain large units of study on the judiciary and civil liberties, both of which are important in many landmark cases, this book could be a well-used resource by the end of a semester. Teachers who teach government courses may have time to use the more in-depth activities in addition to the scenarios and questions that are included with each case.

Whatever the age of the student, and whatever the course, *Supreme Court Decisions* is designed to spark inquiry and discussion while keeping an eye on making the material relevant to students. The activities herein are designed to be fun and engaging for all students.

How to Proceed

After deciding which case you will use, make and hand out copies of the vignette in Section 1. You may make one copy and project for the class to see. Depending on your class, you may want to have them read the vignette aloud so that you can stop them periodically to gauge their understanding, or students can read it silently or in groups. You may want to consider having students look at *context definitions*. Have students underline or highlight unfamiliar words from the text as they read. After they have completed their reading, but before the discussion, give students a few minutes to pair up to discuss difficult words and define them using context clues. This is a good way to have students learn any vocabulary that may be unfamiliar to them.

After reading the vignette, use the discussion questions at the end of the section to help your class think through the case and make predictions about the outcome of the real Supreme Court case. After the discussion, proceed to Section 2. If you want the students to do a follow-up activity, use one of the suggested activities on the following pages or one of your own choosing.

List of Follow-Up Activities

The following activities can be used with any of the cases presented in this book. You may want to offer a variety of activities from which to choose for each case so students can create a product of interest to them, or select certain ones to go along with a case that is being discussed. A few of the cases have an activity included in the teacher pages as an additional idea specific to that particular case.

One idea to help eliminate the need to copy these activities every time a court case is presented is to cut out each activity and laminate it. These cards can be kept in a location in the classroom for students to review as needed as they determine which activity they'd like to complete.

Amicus Curiae Brief

Organizations (e.g., special interest groups, civil rights organizations, the U.S. government) often file *amicus curiae*, or "friends of the court," briefs to be considered in Supreme Court cases.

Prepare a one-page brief outlining an argument for a given position based on the case you have recently discussed. You should consider whether to pick the side of the argument with which you agree or whether you want to challenge yourself to take a more uncomfortable position—arguing for the side with which you may not agree.

Letter to Editor

Write a one-page letter to the editor of a newspaper stating your opinion of the Supreme Court's decision in the case that you just studied. To challenge yourself, you may want to take the point of view with which you actually disagree. See if you can argue the other side in a well-written, coherent letter. Whether you agree or disagree with the Court's ruling, be sure to include facts of the case, as well as specific examples, as you present your opinion. Express your opinion clearly so readers understand your beliefs on the Supreme Court's decision on this case.

DEBATE

A debate is a great way to hear both sides of a case. Your teacher will divide the class into three groups. Group A will present the pro-government position, Group B will present the pro-individual position, and Group C will be the judging panel. Be prepared to discuss this activity upon its conclusion. An outline of the debate is listed below:

- Pick speakers: Groups A and B will each select a primary speaker who may either speak or grant speaking rights to another member of the group for rebuttals.
- Prepare arguments: Groups A and B will have 15 minutes to prepare their arguments; Group C will prepare questions to ask each side after the arguments have been presented.
- Present arguments: The first group (selected by a coin toss) will present its argument. It will have 3 minutes to do so. The second group will then have 3 minutes to present its argument.
- Rebuttals: Each group will have one minute to present a rebuttal. Continue rebuttals for as long as time allows, but for no more than three rounds.
- Panel questions: The judging panel may ask two questions of each group. Group A and Group B each will have one minute to respond to each question.
- Judges deliver a verdict: The judges' decision should be based on content of argument rather than style.

FLOW CHART

Create a flow chart that shows how the case "made it" to the Supreme Court. (You may do this either individually or with a partner.) You may use a computer program to make a neat, legible, and presentable flow chart. In the absence of technology, or if your teacher desires, you may create the flow chart by hand.

The flow chart should include the following elements:

- date and brief description of the original crime or offense;
- names of people and/or organizations involved, including petitioners, respondents, attorneys, justices, and noteworthy friends of the court;
- dates and rulings of the original and appellate courts;
- date the case was argued before the Supreme Court;
- Supreme Court ruling;
- date the Supreme Court released the opinion; and
- a brief statement of the significance of the case.

INTERVIEW

Conduct a taped interview with a person who lived during the time of the Supreme Court case or someone who has extensive knowledge of that particular period of time (e.g., historian, author, college professor). Another option would be to interview someone who works within rules established by the Supreme Court (e.g., police officer). It may be helpful to practice interview techniques with another student before you conduct the interview. The interview should focus on the following elements:

- A brief biography of the person being interviewed, including the person's age and where he or she lived at the time of the case, as well as any other relevant information about him- or herself the person may be willing to discuss.
- The interview should give a sense of (a) what daily life was like, (b) how much the person knew about the case, (c) how controversial the issue was, (d) how people responded to the outcome, (e) how the ruling brought about change, and (f) the effects of the ruling on the interviewee and others.

In addition to the transcript of the interview, you should write a 1–2-page report that not only summarizes the interview, but explains why the interview is significant.

MIND MAPPING

Mind mapping, or concept mapping, is a powerful tool that learners can use to make connections and understand the relationships between concepts. If you do not have experience in mind mapping, the Internet is loaded with resources explaining the benefits of mind maps and how the process works. For more information, a Web site with tutorials can be found at http://www.studygs.net/mapping.

Once you are familiar with the process, create a mind map of the Supreme Court case. Because a mind map is designed to help each individual make connections between concepts, you should do this on your own.

Each mind map should demonstrate an understanding of these basic elements: (a) the Supreme Court decision, (b) the historical context of the decision (i.e., What else was happening at the time?), (c) the political forces at play (e.g., party domination), and (d) the results or aftermath of the decision.

Multimedia Presentation

In a group of 3–5 students, as established by your teacher, you will create a presentation using various media to express how the Supreme Court decision changed society. The presentation can use music, film, video, still photographs, paintings or other artwork, poetry, or other media to show the "before and after" of a Supreme Court case. The easiest way to create such a presentation is probably through the use of Microsoft PowerPoint or other software; however this is not required. The presentation should not include any speaking or explanation because the media chosen should evoke emotional responses that are more powerful than a spoken explanation. Each student in the group should have a specific role that can be assessed.

Your presentation should be 7–10 minutes in length, and your teacher will screen it before it is shown to the class. Regardless of the media you choose, the presentation should demonstrate an understanding of the issues involved, the historical context, and the magnitude of the effects of a particular case. Be creative!

Political Cartoon

Political cartoons provide information on a social or political issue in a humorous or satirical style. These drawings are used to draw attention to certain events or people in the news and often contain the illustrator's opinions or criticisms about the subject. Similar elements can be found in most political cartoons, including exaggerated features or physical characteristics, visual metaphors, and common, recognizable symbols. Examples of political cartoons can be found in the daily newspaper and on the Internet. Review some of these to have a basic understanding of what is included in political cartoons and how they are used to convey an idea or opinion to the reader.

Draw a political cartoon depicting an opinion of the Supreme Court's ruling. Be sure to think about all of the elements that must be present in your cartoon to make it effective.

Research the Court Case

Using resources from the library and Internet, gather research about the Supreme Court case. Be sure to look for reliable, credible resources that provide accurate information on the case. Before beginning your research process, review the list of suggestions below to help narrow your topic of research. If you'd prefer to do something different than one of the ideas listed below, present your idea to your teacher for approval before you begin working. Once you've determined the topic of your research and gathered research, prepare a product (e.g., paper, multimedia presentation, artwork, diagram, play) to share the information you've discovered.

- Diagram how the case proceeded through the court system, from its earliest beginnings to the Supreme Court.
- Determine if the case is still valid (has it been overturned or adjusted by later courts?) and note the significance surrounding its validity.
- Did this Court (same justices or chief justice) rule on any other important cases during its tenure? Explain.
- How is this Court considered among historians (e.g., liberal, conservative)? Cite specific examples.

Simulated Court Hearing

A simulated court hearing provides a good way to see how the Supreme Court works. This will be a simulated court hearing on the Supreme Court case (and may not render the same decision given in the real one). Your teacher will (a) pick five students to act as Supreme Court justices, (b) pick one student to argue for the petitioner, (c) pick one student to argue for the respondent, (d) pick one student to serve as the marshal of the court, and (e) divide the remainder of the class into two groups to write *amicus curiae* briefs (approximately one page in length). This will be assigned the day before the hearing so that the briefs can be submitted to the justices before oral arguments take place.

Procedures:

- Justices will be given *amicus curiae* briefs before oral arguments begin.
- The marshal of the court should call out, "The Honorable Chief Justice and the Associate Justices of the Supreme Court of the United States. Oyez! Oyez! Oyez! All persons having business before the Honorable Supreme Court of the United States are admonished to draw near and give their attention, for the Court is now sitting. God save the United States and this Honorable Court!"
- Justices will be positioned at the front of the class. Shake hands with each other before being seated.
- The petitioner is given 10 minutes to present his or her oral argument. Justices may interrupt and ask questions during this period. The respondent is then given the same amount of time.
- The justices will have the remainder of the class period to render their decision and write a short opinion. If they are split, then each side should write a short, separate opinion.
- As the justices are conferring, the rest of the class will write a prediction of the outcome of the hearing. (Your teacher may prefer to have you discuss this orally if the justices can move to another teacher's classroom or the library as they work on their decision.)
- The opinion will be published (posted on the wall or someplace in the classroom) before the class meets the following day.
- The class will discuss the ruling in a debriefing session.

TELEVISION NEWS REPORT

In a group of 3–4 students, you will present a "television news" feature that describes the Supreme Court decision. Each group member should have a different role (e.g., news anchor, on-the-scene reporter, interview subject, producer, script writer, editor). To make this fun, consider dressing in attire consistent with the times. Don't worry if the case took place after the advent of local television news: It will be great fun for you and entertaining for the class to see you dressed in 1820s garb while doing a TV news program!

Presentations should be approximately 5 minutes in length, and the report should include the following: (a) a description of the court case, (b) an explanation of why the case is significant, (c) a prediction of how the case will change the lives of the viewing audience, and (d) an interview with someone central to the case.

THIS YEAR IN HISTORY

Conduct research on what was taking place during the time period in which the court case occurred. You can locate old magazines or books in the library or go online to use any of the Web sites listed below (or others of your choosing—these Web sites abound) to look at the major news events of that year, popular books and songs, current scientific thought, and the like. You can present your findings to class in either a PowerPoint or other type of visual presentation. The presentation should include the following: (a) information on at least two news events that were important during this time (must be something other than the case itself), (b) information on who was in the White House (along with party affiliation), (c) information on at least two popular items (e.g., sports, songs, movies, books), and (d) most importantly, why these items are significant to know when studying this particular case.

Possible Internet resources:
http://memory.loc.gov/ammem/today/archive.html
http://www.history.com/tdih.do
http://www.brainyhistory.com

Venn Diagram

Create a Venn diagram to compare and contrast two or more selected Supreme Court cases. If you are comparing two cases, there will be two circles with a small overlap. If you are comparing three cases, there will be three circles, each of which will overlap at one point with the other two. You should hand-draw your own Venn diagram or use a computer to generate your own. Just make sure it's neat so that you can use it to study! Each Venn circle should be labeled with a specific Supreme Court case. Each circle should contain at least seven items, three of which overlap with the other case(s). Finally, write a paragraph at the bottom of the page stating why the shared items are significant.

What If?

What if? is a fun way to think about what might have happened had the outcome been different on the Supreme Court case. You will participate in a group of 3–4 students to answer the following question: "What if the Supreme Court had ruled the other way?" Your answer should provide the audience with a glimpse of society under the alternative ruling, suggest how historical events might have been changed, or show how the changes might have altered a person's life.

Your group can present its answer to the question in a way that best fits its response. Some ideas include sketches or illustrations that can be drawn on butcher paper or poster board and a skit or scenario depicting how society or the life of an individual would be different. Finally, you will present your "What if?" to the class in a short presentation. Be prepared for a short debriefing session after all of the groups have presented to discuss what you have learned from the activity.

WHAT WOULD HAPPEN?

This activity asks you to think about what might happen if the Supreme Court case was overturned by the Court today. In a group of 3 or 4 students, discuss what would happen if the present Supreme Court overturned the landmark ruling. Would society be any different? Would our rights be limited or expanded? How might this change affect others in the future? Spend some time brainstorming how things might be different if the Court did overturn the original case and record your ideas. Once you have finished brainstorming, think about how you might share your thoughts with the class. Think of a creative way to show what might happen should the Supreme Court make this change. You should include at least three direct consequences of the ruling and one unintended consequence.

Supreme Court FAQs*

How was the federal court system created?
1. The Supreme Court was established by Article III of the U.S. Constitution.
2. Lower federal courts were created by the Judiciary Act of 1789.

Who sits on the Supreme Court?
1. Nine justices sit on the Supreme Court.
2. The number is established by law, not the Constitution:
     - 1 chief justice
     - 8 associate justices
     - This has been as high as 10 and as low as 6.
     - The Constitution lists no requirements to be a Supreme Court justice; however, modern justices undergo a rigorous confirmation process.

How does one become a Supreme Court justice?
1. Justices are appointed by the President of the United States and confirmed by the Senate.
2. Supreme Court justices serve life terms, unless they resign or are impeached. Only one Supreme Court justice (Samuel Chase) has been impeached, although he was not convicted by the Senate and remained a Supreme Court justice.

What is the Supreme Court's jurisdiction?
1. The court has original jurisdiction (a case is heard for the first time) in these types of cases:
     - cases involving foreign diplomats,
     - U.S. vs. state(s),
     - state(s) vs. state(s),
     - citizen(s) of one state vs. citizen(s) of another state, and
     - state(s) vs. foreign country.
2. The court has appellate jurisdiction (reviews cases already heard) in these types of cases:
     - from the U.S. Courts of Appeal,
     - from the Court of Appeals for the Federal Circuit,
     - from Legislative Courts, and
     - state courts of last resort (e.g., Texas Supreme Court or Texas Court of Criminal Appeals).

How does a case get to the Supreme Court?

1. The losing party in a federal or state court requests an appeal to the Supreme Court through a petition.
2. Justices review these petitions (approximately 7,500 per year) in conference. If four justices wish to hear the case, then the case goes on the schedule, or docket, to be heard (approximately 100 per year).

What happens after the Supreme Court selects a case to review?

1. After the case makes it onto the docket, briefs are filed by both sides, and *amicus curiae* briefs are filed by "friends of the court," or people who are not part of the particular case, but who have some kind of interest in it.
3. The case then proceeds to oral arguments where each sides argues its case before the justices. Each side has precisely 30 minutes to make their argument. The argument may be interrupted frequently by the justices, who may ask questions or make comments at any time. Cases are argued before the court starting in October and lasting into June.
4. After a case is argued, it is discussed in conference where votes are taken and the opinion writing is assigned.
5. The opinion on the case is written and circulated among the justices.
6. Finally, the decision is announced.

What happens after the Supreme Court announces its decision?

This is sometimes the most difficult part—getting a ruling implemented in society. After the court announces its decision, federal, state, and local police agencies; courts; bureaucracies; and institutions must change their policies to abide by and enforce the ruling. For unpopular rulings, this process can take decades. The ruling that ended legal racial segregation, *Brown v. Board of Education* (1954), took almost 20 years to be fully implemented.

* *Note.* Information adapted from Edwards, Wattenberg, and Lineberry (2002).

CASE 1:
THE POWER TO DESTROY
McCulloch v. Maryland (1819)

FOR THE TEACHER

Quick Reference

The Issue: Maryland state officials, unhappy with the existence of the U.S. bank, a competitor to their own chartered banks, levied a state tax against the federal bank. The bank's cashier refused to pay the tax and was subsequently fined by the state of Maryland.

The Players:
James McCulloch—cashier of the Baltimore branch of the Bank of the United States.
Daniel Webster—McCulloch's attorney.
John Marshall—Chief Justice of the Supreme Court.

The Ruling: The court ruled in favor of McCulloch, with Marshall arguing that if a state is allowed to tax the federal government, then it is supreme over the federal government. Thus, it must not be allowed to do so. Or, as he wrote, " . . . the power to tax involves the power to destroy."

Significance: This case firmly established the supremacy of the national government over the states.

Background

The early landmark cases of the Supreme Court were sweeping in nature and laid the foundation for the practical concept of the application of the U.S. Constitution. *Marbury v. Madison* (1803), for example, solidified the court's role in determining the constitutionality of law. That precedent having been set, the Supreme Court settled one constitutional dispute after another. *McCulloch v. Maryland* (1819) is important for several reasons. On its face, it established the dominance of the national government in the federalist system. In the court's ruling, Chief Justice John Marshall noted that a state could not tax a national entity because "the power to tax involves the power to destroy."

On another level, however, this case showcased the power wielded by the president through lifetime appointments to the federal bench. The Federalist Party idea of a strong national government found life not through the democratic process, but through judicial fiat (creating law instead of interpreting it). The Federalist Party was all but dead by 1819, but its ideas of a strong judiciary, powerful central government, and flexible constitution lived on through Supreme Court Justices like John Marshall. The court asserted its own power (not listed in the Constitution) to interpret the Constitution in *Marbury v. Madison* (1803). It solidified the supremacy of the national government over state governments in *McCulloch v. Maryland* (1819). Finally, in *Gibbons v. Ogden* (1824), the court validated the idea that the Constitution is not limited to what is specifically written, but that elements may be inferred by the court. Each of these ideas had been championed by the Federalist Party before its demise, and were at odds with the beliefs of the Democratic-Republicans who presided during this time.

Section 1
The Power to Destroy

June 21, 1819

Dear Robert,

It has been two years, brother, since our last correspondence and I pray this letter finds you healthy. Alas, I have not attended to my letter writing as I promised. I fear these many months have proven most stressful.

Please do not fret over the family, as Emma and Little John are healthy and causing much good-natured havoc around town. Baltimore is growing too, but I fear its havoc is not as good-natured.

Who would have known that my principal woes would have come in the form of assuming the duties of Cashier of the Baltimore branch of the Bank of the United States? I fear my illustrious rise in this institution has only caused me grief, for now I have attained the title Common Criminal! Indeed, I have been convicted by the state of Maryland and am to pay a fine in the sum of two thousand five hundred dollars. I will have to sell my house to pay such a hefty ransom!

And, what did I do to earn this debt to the state? What evil doing brought such woe upon me? Surely you guess that I have embezzled funds, defrauded depositors, or falsified audits. Certainly not! (These petty offenses don't summon the wrath of a $2,500 fine.) What I did was to endeavor to faithfully fulfill the requirements of my position. Thus, when the State of Maryland presented the bank with a tax bill of $15,000, I naturally refused to pay.

Mind you, Robert, this is the Bank of the United States chartered by Congress. The State of Maryland then has the audacity to tax the United States government! Maryland claims to be a sovereign state, but I suspect it is trying to eliminate the competition to its own state-chartered banks.

I tell you that I did not take my conviction and shunting to the criminal class lying down. I have appealed my conviction through the Maryland courts and now await my day before the Supreme Court of the United States! I shall inform you immediately upon news of the ruling.

Until then, I remain your humble brother and servant,

James

Discussion Questions:

1. What is the major issue to be settled by the case?

2. What are the facts relevant to the case?

3. Why do you think the state of Maryland taxed the bank?

4. How do you think the Supreme Court ruled?

5. You be the judge: Should James be forced to pay the fine? Why or why not?

Section 2: The Actual Case
McCulloch v. Maryland (1819)

The establishment of the Bank of the United States was a major source of controversy at the time of its charter in 1791. It was to serve as a place where the national government could deposit funds, issue currency, collect taxes, and so forth. Proponents of the bank, such as Alexander Hamilton, argued that even though the U.S. Constitution did not specifically state that such a bank could be created, it didn't state that a bank could *not* be created either. This argument is said to favor a *loose interpretation* of the Constitution.

Opponents of the bank, including Thomas Jefferson, argued that because the Constitution did not specifically give Congress the power to create a bank, then it was forbidden from doing so. This position requires a *strict interpretation* of the Constitution.

The matter came to a head in 1817 when Maryland (a state that opposed the creation of the Bank of the United States) levied a tax of $15,000 against the bank's branch in Baltimore. James McCulloch, the cashier of the bank, refused to pay the tax and was convicted in state court and fined $2,500. McCulloch appealed the decision all the way to the Supreme Court (Mikula & Mabunda, 1999).

Maryland's lawyers argued that, because the federal government had the authority to tax state banks, Maryland, as a sovereign state, had the authority to tax the federal bank. They also argued that because the Constitution did not specifically give Congress the power to charter a bank, then the bank itself was unconstitutional.

McCulloch's lawyers, one of whom was Daniel Webster, argued that Congress' creation of a national bank was "necessary and proper," as is implied in the Constitution but not specifically stated. He also argued that Maryland's tax hindered the function of federal government (Mikula & Mabunda, 1999).

THE RULING

First, the Supreme Court, led by Chief Justice John Marshall, struck a blow to those with a strict view of the Constitution. Marshall stated that the Constitution gives Congress the power to "lay and collect Taxes; . . . to borrow Money; . . . to regulate Commerce . . ." among other things. (These are known as *enumerated powers* because they are specifically listed in the Constitution.) But, the Constitution also gives Congress the power to make "all Laws which shall be necessary and proper, for carrying into Execution the foregoing Powers . . ." So, even though the Constitution doesn't specifically mention a bank, Marshall argued that the creation of a bank was a necessary and proper function of Congress.

Second, he argued that the states had no authority to tax any institution or function of the federal government. He stated that "the power to tax involves the power to destroy . . ." and that the "American people . . . did not design to make their government dependent upon the states . . ." (*McCulloch v. Maryland* [1819]).

THE AFTERMATH

Thus, the conviction of James McCulloch was overturned by the Supreme Court. Perhaps more important, however, the legitimacy of the *implied* powers became the law of the land and paved the way for a much more flexible, expanding Constitution. However, the argument didn't end here. Elements of this argument between strict and loose interpreters of the Constitution have found their way into the Nullification Crisis, the Civil War, and even into present-day political arguments regarding presidential power, illegal immigration, education, and most notably, reproductive rights.

MAKING IT CURRENT

In the structure of the U.S. military, the National Guard typically is under the command of the governor of the state. However, the U.S. President also has the authority to call National Guard troops to active duty. Do you think it would be legal for the governor of a state to order National Guard troops to resist the orders of a federal court? (This happened in 1957.) How would it be resolved? How does this apply to *McCulloch v. Maryland*?

CASE 2:
THE STEAMBOAT CONTROVERSY
GIBBONS V. OGDEN (1824)

FOR THE TEACHER

Quick Reference

The Issue: The state of New York required a state license to operate a ferry—in this case, to operate between New York and New Jersey. However, the federal government issued licenses to operate in interstate waters. This put the federal and state governments at odds as to which entity had the authority to grant such licenses.

The Players:
Thomas Gibbons—Operated a ferry licensed by the United States.
Aaron Ogden—Operated a ferry licensed by the state of New York. Filed suit against Gibbons.
John Marshall—Chief Justice of the Supreme Court.

The Ruling: New York made Gibbons stop operating the ferry because he didn't hold their license. Gibbons appealed the case to the Supreme Court, which overturned the state's ruling, stating that only the U.S. Congress had the authority to regulate interstate commerce.

Significance: In this case, the court ruled that interstate commerce did not just refer to the buying and selling of goods and services between parties of two or more states. Commerce, according to the court, also referred to any interaction that occurred between states. This greatly increased the reach of Congress, because as the definition of interstate commerce was made expandable, so was the power wielded over it.

Background

   Gibbons v. Ogden (1824) is another of the sweeping early landmark decisions of the Supreme Court. Although it is not a particularly exciting case in terms of human drama, it is important in its effects on the scope of power of the national government. Specifically, its ruling on interstate commerce was just the beginning of the national government's expanding power over business. Throughout the nation's history, the definition of interstate commerce has broadened well beyond the court's ruling in *Gibbons*, but this expanding power started here.

SECTION 1
THE STEAMBOAT CONTROVERSY

Benjamin Bryce opened the door quickly, but still let the harsh winter in with him before pulling it closed against the wind. He trudged into the kitchen of his New York home without bothering to take off his muddy boots and sat down hard at the table where he rested before summoning the energy to light a kerosene lamp. The lamp light on his face exaggerated the lines he'd earned from 30 years of sailing the Hudson River.

"Gracious, Benjamin, you're exhausted." Mary spoke quietly from the darkened hallway door. "A busy day?"

Benjamin rubbed his calloused hands over his face and beard—an attempt at rejuvenation. "Yes. Busy. I spent the morning with lawyers from the state. The rest of the day I spent making up for the lost time."

Benjamin Bryce lived the only life he ever wanted and the only life he ever knew: that of a sailor. His years of toil had made him an expert on the treacherous waters of the Hudson River. He'd worked as a pilot, then as a captain of his own ship, and finally was rewarded with a coveted license, granted by the federal government to provide steamboat service in interstate waters. The work was grueling, often keeping him on the water for days at a time, but he had a good crew. The government did not grant many such licenses. In fact, Benjamin possessed the only one for his area. The result: long days, yes, but they meant a monopoly fortune earned for Benjamin.

Mary Bryce sat down across the table. "Lawyers? Whatever for?"

He pulled a folded sheet of parchment from his breast pocket and flipped it to her across the table. Mary opened the stiff paper carefully and read. After a minute or two she looked up.

"The state of New York is ordering you to stop doing business? How can they do that?"

"The state insists that it has the power to issue licenses to operators in its waters, and I don't have one of those. New York has licensed Joseph Johnston to operate here, not me."

"But, you already have a license . . ." Mary began.

"Of course I do!" he snapped. Then, more calmly, "Of course I do, from the United States herself."

"What did you do Benjamin? What *will* you do?" she asked, worry painted across her face.

"I told them I'd see them in court. Then, I went to work."

Discussion Questions

1. What are the important facts in this case?

2. What is the major question to be settled?

3. Look at Article III of the Constitution. Does it give the Supreme Court the authority to overturn laws?

4. In your opinion, who should have the power to grant licenses in this case? And, to whom should they be granted?

5. You be the judge: Who wins this case? Why?

Section 2: The Actual Case
Gibbons v. Ogden (1824)

Thomas Gibbons was a steamboat ferry owner who operated between New York and New Jersey under the protection of a federal license established by a 1793 law. One of his competitors was Aaron Ogden. Ogden held a state license to operate in the same waters and believed that he should not have any competition because he held a monopoly license (the right to operate without competition).

Ogden filed a complaint with the state of New York arguing that Gibbons was operating illegally in waters in which the state had given Ogden the right to hold a monopoly. The state of New York agreed with Ogden and ordered Gibbons to stop operating. Gibbons appealed this decision to the U.S. Supreme Court (Mikula & Mabunda, 1999).

The Ruling

The Supreme Court, under chief justice John Marshall, ruled that New York overstepped its authority in creating a law that regulated interstate commerce. It would have been ridiculous to have bordering states all require separate licenses and all be able to grant conflicting monopolies for travel up and down or across the same river! Regulation of interstate commerce, according to the Constitution, was a power reserved for Congress. No one really argued that Congress did not hold this power, but rather a key issue was the definition of the word *commerce* itself. As Marshall wrote: ". . . The mind can scarcely conceive a system for regulating commerce between nations, which shall exclude all laws concerning navigation . . ." (*Gibbons v. Ogden* [1824]). The court defined commerce not merely as buying and selling goods (as New York argued), but as *interaction*. Thus, navigation between states is within this broad definition of commerce.

The Aftermath

The Constitution gives Congress the power to regulate interstate commerce, but it does not define the word. This case is important in one sense because it sets a definition to a power established by the Constitution. More important, however, is the result of the Court's definition. Because it defined commerce in terms far beyond just buying and selling of goods, it greatly increased the power of Congress. Now, because of John Marshall's written opinion, interstate commerce could be almost any sort of interstate interaction. This ruling ensured that Congress had the sole power of regulating such interaction. Furthermore, because the ruling broadened the powers of Congress, it also narrowed the powers of individual states in this area.

Making It Current

Who is responsible for passing laws that govern the Internet? Can you think of any problems that might occur if each state had its own Internet laws?

CASE 3:
FREEDOM'S SUIT

DRED SCOTT V. SANDFORD (1857)

FOR THE TEACHER

Quick Reference

The Issue: Dred Scott, a slave, moved with his owner from a slave state to a free state and then back to a slave state. He sued his owner for his freedom on the grounds that he should have been freed when living in the free state.

The Players:
Dred Scott—Slave who sued for his freedom.
Roger B. Taney—Supreme Court Justice writing the majority opinion. Avid state's rights advocate and supporter of slavery.
Dr. and Mrs. Emerson—Scott's masters who failed to grant Scott's freedom in Wisconsin, a free state, and denied his freedom upon return to Missouri, a slave state.

The Ruling: Because Scott was Black, and therefore not a citizen, he had no standing to sue in court. The court also ruled that the Missouri Compromise was unconstitutional.

Significance: The ruling outraged northern abolitionists and helped to deeply divide the country regarding racial issues. Furthermore, the ruling on the Missouri Compromise set the stage for the violence that occurred in Kansas, sometimes referred to as "Bleeding Kansas." Both of these effects sped up the arrival of the Civil War.

Background

Dred Scott v. Sandford is arguably the most pivotal case in our nation's history. Some historians consider the incredible ruling (that people of African descent were not citizens and thus could not sue in court) the event that virtually guaranteed that the nation would split into factions and that ultimately led to the Civil War. Today, the ruling is considered so indefensible that it seems shocking to us that the Supreme Court could ever make it. Beyond helping to start the Civil War, it also set solidly into law the notion that Blacks were an inferior class. The issue was only settled after a bloody civil war, three amendments to the Constitution, and a century of civil rights protests, legislation, and judicial rulings.

SECTION I
FREEDOM'S SUIT

"You're tellin' me I'm a free man?" Daniel asked softly. "*We're* free?"

He pulled his new bride Nell closer to him, his arm around her waist. William, his newest friend, only nodded. Daniel's face lit up, cracking into a hundred leathery wrinkles as he grinned broadly—a sight Nell had seldom seen.

"But, be careful," William warned, "remember where you are. You may supposed to be free, but you ain't yet."

Daniel's face fell back to its normal stoic expression when he realized his friend was right. *If* he was really a free man, he was still in Missouri and the law didn't do much to protect a Black man.

That night, Daniel and Nell Johnson discussed the possibilities that lay before them. They were too smart to allow themselves much excitement, but the prospect of freedom gave Daniel a sense of pride he'd never before felt. "We got to talk to Miz Perry," Daniel said.

Nell disagreed. "Why don't we just go if we're already free?"

"If we just go we'll be chased down like dogs," Daniel said. "Then that's it for us."

Nell nodded her head solemnly, "You should talk to her tomorrow."

The next morning, Daniel approached Beatrice Perry, widow of a U.S. Army Colonel. Daniel stood holding his hat in his gnarled hands and looked at his feet as he spoke. "Miz Perry, I've been with you and Colonel Perry, before he died, going on 30 years now . . ."

Beatrice Perry nodded patiently. "Yes, Daniel."

"I went with the colonel to Illinois and I went with him to Wisconsin and all that time I served him well."

"Yes, you've been a good servant." Her patience was wearing thin.

"Well, Miz Perry, I didn't know it at the time but when I went with the colonel up north, they don't allow no slaves up there. I'm supposed to be a free man."

Beatrice Perry's voice turned to iron. "But, you're not up north anymore, Daniel, you're in Missouri. Now, go back to work."

"But Miz Perry, the law says I'm free."

The widow started to turn away when Daniel tried one more thing.

"Miz Perry, how much would I fetch on the block?"

"I don't know Daniel," she said dismissively. "I'm not a slave trader."

"Miz Perry, Nell and I saved $332. I'll give it all to you."

Beatrice Perry looked at Daniel for a moment, then replied, "Go back to work, Daniel. You're not for sale."

Daniel thought about running away, but his mind kept coming back to the law. I shouldn't have to run, he thought. How can the law say I'm free, but yet I'm still a slave? His only course of action now, he figured, was to use the law against his master and file a suit to gain his freedom.

Discussion Questions

1. What is the major question to be settled in this case?

2. What are the facts relevant to the case?

3. The story suggests that the state of Missouri wouldn't protect a legally freed slave. How could this happen?

4. You be the judge: How would you rule in this case? Why?

5. How do you think the Supreme Court ruled?

Section 2: The Actual Case
Dred Scott v. Sandford (1857)

Dred Scott was a slave who had been taken to the free states of Illinois and Wisconsin by his master, army surgeon Dr. John Emerson. Scott married and lived in Wisconsin until Dr. Emerson was moved to Missouri, a slave state. Scott and his wife moved to Missouri with Emerson upon his summons. It wasn't until Emerson died and his widow assigned Scott to an army captain that Scott sued for his freedom.

In 1850, the St. Louis State Circuit Court ruled that Scott was free. However, the Missouri Supreme Court overturned this decision. Scott took his case to a federal court, which upheld the decision of the Missouri Supreme Court. Finally, with no other alternative, Scott appealed his case to the U.S. Supreme Court (PBS Online, 1998).

The Ruling

The ruling was handed down in 1857, and the majority opinion was written by Chief Justice Roger B. Taney, a strong supporter of slavery. The ruling stated that because Dred Scott was Black, he was not a citizen and therefore had no standing to sue anyone. The ruling also declared the Compromise of 1820 (known as the Missouri Compromise) unconstitutional. The Missouri Compromise had established that for every slave state that was admitted to the Union, a free state also must be admitted. This created a balance of power between pro- and antislavery forces and held off armed conflict between the two groups for many years. When the Supreme Court struck it down, it removed one of the major obstacles that prevented a civil war (History Place, 1996).

THE AFTERMATH

This ruling was highly favored by slave states and slave owners, but Northern states and abolitionists were outraged. The decision has been considered a calamity of justice and helped drive the wedge deeper into the fractured nation, ultimately leading it closer to civil war. Dred Scott and his family were later purchased by a former master's children and set free.

MAKING IT CURRENT

The ruling in the case of Dred Scott was based on a belief in racial superiority. What strides has the United States made in accepting the racial diversity of people here and abroad?

CASE 4:
THE CONFEDERATE SYMPATHIZER
EX PARTE MILLIGAN (1866)

FOR THE TEACHER

Quick Reference

The Issue: President Lincoln suspended the writ of habeas corpus during the Civil War in Union states. Many cases were heard by military tribunal rather than civilian courts. In this case, a confederate sympathizer in Indiana was convicted by military tribunal of treason and sentenced to execution.

The Players:
Lambdin P. Milligan—A civilian Confederate sympathizer who collected arms and plotted to attack union installations.

The Ruling: The court ruled that the president could not suspend civilian courts in areas where the insurrection did not disrupt their ability to function. Because Indiana was not physically affected by the war, then civilian courts should have tried the case of Milligan, a civilian. The court overturned the conviction.

Significance: The case set clear boundaries of executive power, especially during time of war.

Background

Ex Parte Milligan is an important case, not only because it showed the Court's willingness to limit presidential authority, but also because of present-day ramifications. The ruling, which set clear limits on the president's power to suspend habeas corpus, bears reviewing in times when presidents are most likely to exercise their wartime powers. The notions of civilian courts, military tribunals, and enemy combatants, which are interspersed throughout *Milligan*, are again at the forefront of President George W. Bush's policies in adjudicating suspects in the "War on Terror." Any discussion of *Ex Parte Milligan* would be incomplete without a review of recent rulings such as *Hamdan v. Rumsfeld* (2006), which also limited the president's use of military tribunals, even in time of war.

Suggested Activity Specific to *Ex Parte Milligan*

Have students research *Hamdan v. Rumsfeld* (2006) and write a brief essay comparing and contrasting it to *Ex Parte Milligan*. How is this case similar to *Ex Parte Milligan*? How is it different?

Section 1
The Confederate Sympathizer

Alfred Vanderjack flinched again, this time hard enough to hit the back of his head on the stone wall to which his iron bed was anchored. Union army guards were testing the gallows that were a permanent fixture just outside of his cell, and he considered this cruel and unusual punishment. Every sound, from the lever mechanism, to the swinging trap door, to the sandbags hitting the end of the rope, reverberated through the stone wall and his bones as he sat on his slab of a bed. Worst of all, he knew his time to hang from the end of that rope was drawing near. A loud rap on his door caused him to flinch again and he cursed under his breath.

The guard, a Union army corporal, opened the door just long enough for Vanderjack's lawyer, Douglas James, to enter the dark, cramped cell.

"Can't you get me away from these gallows?" Vanderjack complained. "What do I pay you for?"

James sat on the edge of the bed and stared for a moment at his client. Finally, he spoke in short, measured tones. "You pay me for this: I believe I have found a basis for an appeal in your case."

"Other than the fact that I am an innocent man . . ." Vanderjack interrupted.

"Yes, other than that."

Vanderjack's continued assertion that he was innocent was beginning to wear on James; both men knew that he had, in fact, committed the crimes for which he was charged. James believed beyond a doubt that Vanderjack had indeed made plans to attack the Union army armory in his home state of Ohio, a Union state. Vanderjack had made no secret of his pro-Confederate leanings through his numerous lengthy and outrageous letters to newspaper editors.

James also knew that Vanderjack had amassed a large number of rifles, ammunition, and powder. And, perhaps worst of all, he had recruited other Confederate sympathizers to join him in his planned attack. Truly Vanderjack was guilty of conspiring to commit treason, a crime punishable by death. The fact that Vanderjack continued to issue false protests of his conviction, even after the mountain of evidence was presented against him, bothered James. James was the defense attorney, however, and his job was to fight for his client, guilty or not.

"When Lincoln suspended habeas corpus," James explained, "that gave the government the authority to arrest you without formal charges . . ."

"That criminal ape, Lincoln . . ." Vanderjack interrupted.

James held up his hand, demanding silence before he would continue. "Lincoln may have had the legal authority to arrest you for no cause, but when the war ended you were tried by a military tribunal instead of a civil court."

"Yes, how is that important?" Vanderjack gave James attention as if life depended on it.

"Ohio's civilian courts never shut down. There was no reason to try you in a military court—you are a civilian, not a soldier."

Alfred Vanderjack stroked his chin and smiled. He might get away from those gallows after all.

Discussion Questions

1. What are the facts pertinent to this case?

2. Does the fact that Vanderjack was tried by a military tribunal rather than a civilian court outweigh his obvious guilt?

3. You be the judge: Must Vanderjack complete the sentence (death) or should he be released? Explain your answer.

4. Does this case have any application in the present day? Explain your response.

Section 2: The Actual Case
Ex Parte Milligan (1866)

During the Civil War, Lambdin P. Milligan and four other men were accused of planning to steal Union army weapons and break into Union prisoner of war camps. This took place in Indiana, a Union state. Prior to this offense, President Abraham Lincoln had suspended the writ of habeas corpus, which means that the military then had the right to arrest and hold "prisoners of war, spies, or aiders and abettors of the enemy" (Mount, 2001). When a president suspends habeas corpus, he is basically declaring martial law; that is, the military has the responsibility to keep law and order, as well as try criminal cases.

Milligan's case was heard in 1864 in a military court, where he was found guilty and condemned to die. Before his execution, however, the war ended and he had the opportunity to appeal his case in a civilian court on the grounds that the entire process behind his conviction was unconstitutional.

The Ruling

The Supreme Court decided to hear the case, and against the dissent of Chief Justice Salmon P. Chase, overturned Milligan's conviction. The court reasoned that martial law could only be put into effect if the state or location had been invaded by hostile forces. Because the state of Indiana had not been invaded, and because its civilian courts were operating normally, then there was no basis for declaring martial law. And, because there should have been no martial law and because Milligan was a civilian, it was unconstitutional to try the case in a military court. In fact, the court called the use of a military tribunal in this case "a gross usurpation of power" (*Ex Parte Milligan*, 1866).

The Aftermath

Since the attack on the World Trade Center on September 11, 2001, the question of trying suspects in military courts has once again surfaced. The court has continued to hold tight restrictions on the use of military tribunals for nonmilitary defendants in cases such as *Hamdan v. Rumsfeld* (2006), which set clearer limits on the president's power to create military tribunals.

Making It Current

Do you believe that members of al-Qaida or other terrorist organizations who have "declared war" on the U.S. should be tried by military or civilian courts? Why does this make a difference?

CASE 5:
THE OUT-OF-PLACE PASSENGER

PLESSY V. FERGUSON (1896)

FOR THE TEACHER

Quick Reference

The Issue: The state of Louisiana required that railroads provide and enforce separate passenger compartments for Black and White passengers.

The Players:
Homer Plessy—Challenged the law by deliberately sitting in a rail car for Whites only in order to get arrested. By getting arrested, he could challenge the law in court.

The Ruling: The court ruled that states could require separate facilities for Blacks and Whites as long as those facilities were equal. This doctrine is known as "separate but equal."

Significance: By allowing states to establish laws separating the races (known as Jim Crow laws), Southern states were free to create White-only establishments, restaurants, schools, busses, drinking fountains, and so forth, and keep Black Americans in an oppressed state for decades to come.

Background

Plessy v. Ferguson (1896) is the second landmark case, after *Dred Scott v. Sandford* (1857), that constituted an enormous setback for Black Americans. The *Plessy* decision might not have been as blatantly bigoted as the ruling in *Dred Scott*, but it caused similar catastrophic results. The idea that two races could be kept separate and be called equal was faulty thinking in the extreme. In fact, the ruling paved the way for Jim Crow laws, that kept Black Americans as second-class citizens for the next 60 years. It wasn't until such rulings as *Sweatt v. Painter* (1950) and *Brown v. Board of Education of Topeka* (1954; which will be discussed in detail later in the book), that the walls of legal segregation began to be torn down. Unfortunately, the specter of segregation was not as easily eliminated as changing the law, for segregated communities already were long-established. To try to get those communities together in schools would require more wrenching upheaval in the form of bussing (*Swann v. Charlotte-Mecklenburg Board of Education*, 1971).

SECTION 1
THE OUT-OF-PLACE PASSENGER

Jesse Donner held his breath as he stepped onto the train. He had prepared for this day for weeks, but he still hoped in his heart that he would not be stopped. He hoped that just this one time a man's heritage wouldn't determine where he could live, eat, or even sit on a train. He walked down the aisle empty handed; no luggage in his hand. It wasn't necessary because he didn't plan on riding the train for long.

Jesse looked around at the White faces as he passed through the first car. Interesting, he thought, that no one even gave him a second look. They'd notice him soon enough. Jesse continued to the next passenger car and was surprised to see it already filling up, only the faces he saw in this car were Black, although he did not recognize anyone. Jesse stopped, took a deep breath, turned around and walked back toward the front, his heart racing now.

When Jesse entered the White car this time, he drew the attention of several passengers. This time their faces registered the look of annoyance. Some even sighed large breaths of exasperation. Why did this man have to come back into their car? Jesse looked each of them in the eye as they stared at him silently. Finally, Jesse stopped at an empty aisle seat and abruptly sat down and held his gaze straight ahead, his head held high.

Then, the grumbling started, low at first, but it grew louder the longer Jesse stayed seated. He kept his eyes to the front, though, even when some of the passengers reminded him, loudly, that he was in the wrong car. It seemed to Jesse that he sat in that seat for an eternity, but now he was in this and he was not going to move. He also knew that he must not allow his anger to get the better of him. Even if someone became physical with him or assaulted him, he knew that any physical attempt to protect himself would be used against him and would disrupt his plan.

He was afraid for a moment that he would be tested in this regard when a large man grabbed him by the arm, shouting at him with a spitting, angry contorted face. Jesse just gritted his teeth and held on to his seat. Luckily, the conductor ran to Jesse's seat and calmed down the man. The train would not leave, he assured the passengers, until this situation was in hand.

Finally, a transit policeman boarded the train and calmly told Jesse to stand. Jesse did what he was told, but did not speak. The policeman put handcuffs on Jesse and led him peacefully from the train. When they stepped onto the loading platform, a man emerged from the crowd and identified himself to the policeman as Jesse's lawyer. He followed Jesse to the police station, where Jesse was processed and put in jail for breaking the state law that required Black passengers to ride in separate passenger cars from White passengers.

Discussion Questions

1. What are the facts that are pertinent to this case?

2. What arguments do you predict will be used by each side in the real court case?

3. Why was Jesse so nervous getting on the train, and why was his lawyer waiting for him to disembark?

4. What is the major question to be decided by this case?

5. You be the judge: Did Jesse have the right to sit in the passenger car with the White passengers?

6. How do you think the Supreme Court ruled?

Section 2: The Actual Case
Plessy v. Ferguson (1896)

In the 1890s, the state of Louisiana passed a law requiring that all passenger trains operating in the state provide "separate but equal" compartments for Black and White passengers. This could take the form of separate passenger cars or partitions that separated Black and White passengers. In 1892, Homer Plessy (who was one-eighth Black) challenged the Separate Car Act, as the law was known, by riding in the Whites-only passenger car of the East Louisiana Railroad Company (Sanson, 1999).

Plessy's challenge, however, was not a spur-of-the-moment protest. It had been carefully orchestrated by a civil rights group with the assistance of the East Louisiana Railroad Company itself. The civil rights group, the Citizens' Committee to Test the Constitutionality of the Separate Car Act, planned for Plessy's arrest so that the question would get into the court system. Only then could the case possibly make it to the Supreme Court, where its constitutionality could be determined (Sanson, 1999).

The Ruling

Plessy was arrested, as planned, but a Louisiana court, presided over by Judge John Howard Ferguson, ruled that a "separate car" law was unconstitutional only if the trains were passing through different states. However, the law could apply to trains that stayed within the state of Louisiana. Thus, the law was upheld as constitutional. Plessy appealed the ruling to the Louisiana Supreme Court, where the law again was upheld as constitutional.

Finally, Plessy appealed the state's ruling to the U.S. Supreme Court, which heard the case now titled *Plessy v. Ferguson* (naming the judge in the original case.) In a crushing blow to Plessy and civil rights, the Supreme Court ruled that Louisiana's Separate Car Act was indeed constitutional (Sanson, 1999).

The majority opinion, written by Justice Henry Brown, stated that the law violated neither the Thirteenth Amendment (prohibiting slavery) nor the Fourteenth Amendment (requiring equal treatment under the law). He wrote,

> The object of the [Fourteenth] amendment was undoubtedly to enforce the absolute equality of the two races before the law, but in the nature of things it could not have been intended to abolish distinctions based upon color, or to enforce social, as distinguished from political, equality, or a commingling of the two races upon terms unsatisfactory to either. (*Plessy v. Ferguson* [1896])

The Aftermath

The dissenting opinion, written by Justice John Marshall Harlan, predicts with chilling accuracy the outcome of the *Plessy v. Ferguson* decision:

> What can more certainly arouse race hate, what more certainly create and perpetuate a feeling of distrust between these races, than state enactments which, in fact, proceed on the ground that colored citizens are so inferior and degraded that they cannot be allowed to sit in public coaches occupied by white citizens? (*Plessy v. Ferguson* [1896])

The *Plessy* decision paved the way for states to pass more laws (known as Jim Crow laws) requiring the separation of races in restaurants, theaters, schools, public transportation, and buildings under the banner of "separate but equal." It also fanned the fires of racial hatred that created groups like the Ku Klux Klan that terrorized Black citizens for decades (and still exist to this day). The segregation of Blacks and Whites in America in the 20th century is a direct result of the Supreme Court's ruling in *Plessy v. Ferguson*, and was not legally overturned until 1954. In practice, however, the walls of segregation stayed in place for almost 70 years.

Making It Current

Have you seen evidence of racial segregation in your town? Are there neighborhoods that consist almost entirely of people of one race or another? Is there ever a point when the government should step in to change something like this?

Case 6:
The Instigator

Schenck v. U.S. (1919)

For the Teacher

Quick Reference

The Issue: What forms of speech are protected by the First Amendment? In this case, an antiwar protester published a pamphlet urging men to resist the draft (for service in World War I).

The Players:
Charles Schenck—Antiwar protester who argued against Americans serving in World War I on the grounds that it constituted involuntary servitude and was a violation of the Thirteenth Amendment. Convicted of violating the Espionage Act of 1917.
Oliver Wendell Holmes—Chief Justice of the Supreme Court.

The Ruling: The Supreme Court upheld Schenck's conviction.

Significance: Set clear limits on what constituted free speech. Holmes wrote that speech that represented a clear and present danger was not protected by the First Amendment.

Background

Schenck v. U.S. marks this book's first coverage of the Court's many 20th-century rulings regarding the rights of individuals protected by the Bill of Rights. *Schenck* is important because it set an early standard regarding the First Amendment. Here, Justice Holmes' famous "clear and present danger" test was offered as the threshold for when speech becomes unprotected. Even though the clear and present danger test was soon altered, Holmes' statement that the First Amendment "would not protect a man in falsely shouting fire in a theatre . . ." has stood as a common-sense measure of the limits to an individual's freedom of speech. After *Schenck,* the court issued many opinions on all aspects of the First Amendment including the following:

- freedom of speech,
- freedom of the press,
- freedom of assembly,
- free exercise of religion,
- establishment of religion, and
- freedom of association.

SECTION I
THE INSTIGATOR

Dan Rowan took a deep breath before swinging open the mahogany doors leading in to the plush office. To Rowan, the heft of the door represented the reputation of the man whose office he was entering. Johnson Groves, the United States Attorney for the District of New York, came from behind his massive desk and offered his hand warmly when Rowan entered the room.

"Agent Rowan, I'm John Groves. I believe you and I met last year at your induction. Nice to see you again."

"Yes, sir." Rowan's voice cracked as he said it. He made up for the squeak by squeezing Groves' hand firmly and giving it a vigorous shake. Groves smiled with bemused confidence and offered Rowan a seat in a polished leather chair.

"Agent Rowan," Groves began after both men were seated, "tell me about this Schmidt."

"Well, sir, a Hoboken cop gave this to one of our agents who gave it to me." Rowan pulled a folded pamphlet from his briefcase and handed it over to Groves. "Schmidt is distributing this flier to men all over Hoboken and Newark." Rowan continued, "He is also the author. I think his words tell you all you need to know."

Groves read the pamphlet aloud in a theatrical tone.

Countrymen, oppose the draft!

Be not a pawn for the moneyed interests of Wall Street.

The Great War in Europe is not our fight!

> The Great War in Europe has been perpetrated by the dynasties and is fought out by the pawns of Europe and America.

> The Great War in Europe has cost the lives of hundreds of thousands of us, but none of the scions of the European dynasties!

Oppose the draft!

Your conscription violates the Thirteenth Amendment of the U.S. Constitution by forcing involuntary servitude!

Petition against the Conscription Act!

Oppose the draft!

Groves placed the flier carefully on his desk and rubbed his temples. "You're looking to arrest this man, Agent Rowan?"

"Yes, sir. But, I wanted the opinion of the U.S. Attorney's office before I even tried for a warrant."

"Clearly this Schmidt is exercising his First Amendment right to free speech, wouldn't you agree?"

"There's a war on sir, I think that changes everything."

Groves considered the argument. "You may be right," Groves allowed, "but there's sure to be a court battle if we arrest him. This pamphlet is carefully worded to avoid a call to arms."

"There's a war on, sir. This represents a clear violation of the Espionage Act."

Johnson Groves considered the argument before giving his answer.

Discussion Questions

1. Based on what you've learned about the constitution, do you think arresting Schmidt violated his First Amendment right to free speech?

2. You be the judge: Would you sign an arrest warrant for Schmidt? Why or why not?

3. If a court battle ensued, which side do you think would win, the side favoring free speech or the side favoring national security?

4. Are there any current day applications for this case?

5. Do you think a military draft violates the Thirteenth Amendment, which prohibits involuntary servitude (slavery)? Explain your answer.

Section 2: The Actual Case
Schenck v. U.S. (1919)

Charles Schenck was a socialist who spoke out against World War I and the draft in 1917. He argued, through a flyer he wrote and distributed in Philadelphia, that the draft was a violation of the Thirteenth Amendment of the Constitution, which prohibited slavery. Being drafted to fight in a war in which one does not believe, he argued, represented involuntary servitude.

In his pamphlet, he urged those against the war and against the draft to take up peaceful means, such as petitioning and voting out pro-war politicians, to make their opinions heard. He was arrested for conspiracy to violate the Espionage Act of 1917 by hindering military efforts and interrupting recruitment (*Schenck v. U.S.* [1919]).

The Ruling

The U.S. Supreme Court upheld Schenck's arrest and conviction as constitutional and set an important threshold in what constitutes free speech. The decision was unanimous and its opinion was written by Justice Oliver Wendell Holmes, Jr. "[w]hen a nation is at war many things that might be said in time of peace are such a hindrance to its effort that their utterance will not be endured so long as men fight, and that no Court could regard them as protected by any constitutional right" (*Schenck v. U.S.* [1919]).

Holmes also set forth his famous "clear and present danger" threshold. He stated that speech that presented a clear and present danger would not be protected by the First Amendment. Additionally, Holmes used the argument that the First Amendment "would not protect a man in falsely shouting fire in a theatre and causing a panic" (*Schenck v. U.S.* [1919]). Schenck's conviction was upheld and he spent 6 months in prison for his crime.

The Aftermath

As time passed, the court became much more protective of the right to free speech. In the case *Brandenburg v. Ohio* (1969), the Court ruled that in order for speech to be punished, it must not be merely inflammatory or dangerous, but that it must incite "imminent lawless action." For example, a man shouting to a crowd to take up arms against the government could not be punished. However, if the man pointed to a stack of rifles and directed the angry crowd to go shoot at the Capitol, then this might represent incitement of imminent lawless action.

Making It Current

Does the government have the right to punish a blogger for stating the opinion that the government should be overthrown? Should it punish the publisher of a Web site that shows how to make bombs using household items? Where would you draw the line?

CASE 7:
THE PUBLISHER

GITLOW V. NEW YORK (1925)

FOR THE TEACHER

Quick Reference

The Issue: Are states restricted from passing laws which conflict with the Bill of Rights in the U.S. Constitution?

The Players:
Benjamin Gitlow—Convicted by the state of New York for violating the state's law against promoting anarchy. Argued that this law violated his right to free speech guaranteed by the U.S. Constitution.

The Ruling: The Court ruled that language in the Fourteenth Amendment required the states to abide by the federal guarantee of the freedom of speech.

Significance: The ruling reversed the precedent set by *Barron v. Baltimore* (1833), which held that states were not bound by the federal Bill of Rights. It established the *incorporation doctrine*, which would be used for decades to slowly tie the states to many of the guarantees offered by the Bill of Rights.

Background

Gitlow v. New York was selected for this book because it is the real beginning of the *incorporation doctrine* in Supreme Court rulings. Prior to *Gitlow*, the Bill of Rights was considered to restrain only the national government and not the states—a doctrine that was upheld in *Barron v. Baltimore* (1833). In *Gitlow*, the Supreme Court reversed *Barron v. Baltimore* and in so doing tied the states to the Bill of Rights with rope provided by the Fourteenth Amendment. The Fourteenth Amendment's due process clause states that "No . . . State (shall) deprive any person of life, liberty, or property, without due process of law." In *Gitlow*, the Court reasoned that the freedom of speech is a basic liberty and, as such, is included in the scope of the Fourteenth Amendment. (For example, prior to *Gitlow*, the U.S. Congress could not pass a law limiting the freedom of speech, but a state legislature might. After *Gitlow*, neither the federal nor state governments could pass laws limiting free speech.)

The significance of the incorporation doctrine is that it has allowed the Supreme Court, over the years, to offer guarantees to individual liberty that might not have been protected by the states. Also important, the Supreme Court has never incorporated the entire Bill of Rights, but has instead elected to invoke this doctrine piecemeal over many years.

The incorporation doctrine is a concept that often is difficult to grasp for some students. However, it is crucial in understanding the Court's role in protecting individual liberties in the 20th century.

SECTION 1
THE PUBLISHER

The tall, slender man looked up and down the street before descending the stairs to the basement apartment below. He knocked twice quietly, opened the door and slipped inside. The room was dark, as usual, and the air was heavy with cigarette smoke and the smell of binding glue. The man stood for a moment just inside the door waiting for his eyes to adjust before moving. He had to walk carefully to avoid the stacks of boxes and books that covered the small area. When he got to the back office he found the door locked so he knocked again. Finally the door flew open, revealing an aging man already shuffling back to his desk, his white hair aglow in the dimly lit room.

"This is going to get you arrested," the white-haired man said, holding up the inch-thick handwritten manuscript. He offered no handshake and gave no introduction.

"Don't give me that," the slender man said, "it's good and you know it."

"I didn't say it wasn't good—I said it would get you arrested." The old man lit another cigarette and squinted through the smoke.

"I have my rights," the slender man countered.

"You have the right to suggest the violent overthrow of the government?" he coughed.

"I have the right to freedom of speech. It's in a little thing called the Constitution."

"You think the Constitution is going to protect an anarchist?" the white-haired man laughed.

"The Constitution is written to protect unpopular speech, not popular speech. That was one thing they got right." The slender man was beginning to sound preachy.

"Well, you seem to know a whole lot about the government that you are wanting to overthrow, and I guess you should. But, I publish a lot of this stuff, and maybe you ought to know more about a little thing called state law. You see, the State of Massachusetts frowns on this kind of thing." The old man held up the smudged pages again to make his point.

"What do you mean *the State of Massachusetts?*" the slender man asked.

"I mean, it doesn't matter what the U.S. Constitution says," the old man explained. "The U.S. Constitution says that '*Congress* shall make no law abridging the freedom of speech'—it doesn't say a thing about the State of Massachusetts."

"That's not right!" the slender man cried, his face reddening.

"Don't worry, I'll still print it for you, but your name's on it and you'll be the one going to jail."

"Don't worry about me," the slender man said, "you just print my book and I'll worry about the rest. There is no way they can arrest me for it, I have my rights guaranteed by the Constitution. I'll fight it!"

The slender man took a tightly wrapped roll of money out of his pocket and handed it to the white-haired man. The white-haired man took the money and said, "Don't say I didn't warn you."

Discussion Questions

1. Do you think a state can pass a law that violates a right guaranteed by the U.S. Constitution? Explain your answer.

2. Which man from the vignette above do you think is correct in his beliefs? Explain your answer.

3. Do you think the slender man should be arrested? Why or why not?

4. Do you think that a book suggesting the overthrow of the government is protected by the First Amendment? Why or why not?

Section 2: The Actual Case
Gitlow v. New York (1925)

Benjamin Gitlow was a Socialist who wrote the "Left Wing Manifesto," in which he advocated the violent overthrow of the U.S. government. He was convicted of violating New York's Criminal Anarchy law. He appealed the decision by making two different arguments: First, he argued that his writing did not constitute a "clear and present danger" to public safety, the threshold having been determined in 1919 by the Supreme Court in *Schenck v. U.S.* Second, he argued that his arrest violated the Fourteenth Amendment (*Gitlow v. New York* [1925]).

The Ruling

Gitlow's lawyers lost on the first point in which they argued that his speech should have been protected by the First Amendment. The Supreme Court ruled that the nature of Gitlow's publication was so potentially destructive that it posed an imminent threat to the country, even though his writing was nonspecific and mainly rhetorical. Thus, it upheld his conviction as constitutional. More significant, however, was the position the Court took on the meaning of the Fourteenth Amendment.

In the *Gitlow* ruling, the Court stated that the Fourteenth Amendment's due process clause ("nor shall any State deprive any person of life, liberty, or property, without due process of law . . .") bound the individual states to adhere to portions of the First Amendment of the Constitution of the United States. This ruling overturned the previous doctrine established by *Barron v. Baltimore* a century before, which ruled that states were not bound by the U.S. Constitution.

The Aftermath

With *Gitlow v. New York*, the aftermath is arguably far more important than the case itself. The notion that states must provide the protections guaranteed by the U.S. Constitution forever changed the balance of power between the states and the federal government. The concept, known as the *incorporation doctrine*, started with *Gitlow* and tied only the freedoms of speech and press to the states. However, once that precedent was set, the court slowly began incorporating most of the other freedoms guaranteed by the Bill of Rights, as well. Civil liberties became more and more protected from states, as well as the federal government, throughout the 20th century. Accordingly, the power of the Supreme Court to rule in cases involving civil liberties and state laws grew tremendously, as well.

Making It Current

Do you think that a state could pass a law banning handguns? (The second amendment to the U.S. constitution guarantees the right to keep and bear arms.)

CASE 8:
INTO THE CAMP

KOREMATSU v. U.S. (1944)

FOR THE TEACHER

Quick Reference

The Issue: During World War II, the U.S. government required the relocation and internment of Japanese Americans. The issue here was whether the government could hold a group of people based on their race, and not based on actual suspicion of criminal activity.

The Players:
Fred Korematsu—Convicted of defying the executive order to move to a military area. Argued that he was under no suspicion of illegal activity and was being moved solely based on his ancestry.
Hugo Black—Justice who wrote the majority opinion for the Court.

The Ruling: The court upheld Korematsu's conviction on the basis that protection against espionage (especially in time of war) outweighs the rights of an individual.

Significance: The internment of Japanese Americans is considered a calamity of justice by many. The U.S. government even paid restitution to survivors of the internment and admitted that the practice was wrong. Ironically, the Supreme Court has never overturned the decision, so the practice is still considered (technically) constitutional.

Background

Any study of modern U.S. history would be incomplete without an examination of the treatment of Japanese Americans during World War II. Students often are shocked to learn that honest, hard-working citizens were rounded up and moved to relocation camps at the order of the U.S. President. Compounding their shock is the fact that during this time many of the Japanese Americans' family members were fighting bravely for the American cause overseas. It is difficult for students to imagine the level of hysteria created by the combination of the Japanese attack on Pearl Harbor, the ensuing war, and a long-standing distrust on the part of many White Americans toward their Asian counterparts.

Equally troubling is the fact that when presented with the opportunity to overturn the legality of this executive order, the Supreme Court has never actually done so, despite the admission by the U.S. government that the action was wrong (Street Law & The Supreme Court Historical Society, 2002b). As with *Ex Parte Milligan* (1866), the concerns of espionage on the World War II home front parallels the current battle being waged in the "War on Terror."

Suggested Activity Specific to Korematsu v. U.S.

One example of a debate question that might be used for *Korematsu v. U.S.* is "Should the rights of an individual be limited in the government's fight against terrorism or espionage?"

SECTION 1
INTO THE CAMP

It is a cool morning when your mother awakens you before dawn with the simple words, "It's time." You get up quickly, and dress silently for what you fear will be the worst day of your life. Your mother admonishes you to make your bed and you obey, although you really don't know why it's necessary now. You get your little sister out of bed and help her dress and brush her teeth. Your family sits down for a quick bite of bread and the remains of a bottle of milk before your father leads your family of four out the front door. You take one last look at the house in which you grew up and your mother pulls at your dress to get you moving.

Before you even get to the end of the block, your arms are burning from carrying two heavy suitcases, but you are 12 now and you are expected to carry your load. Your sister has already started to whine but your parents only lead on in silence, heads held high. Your family falls into line with the others in your neighborhood who have been told to leave. You want to drop the suitcases and run, but to do so would bring dishonor to your family. Fleeing is not an option.

You and hundreds of others like you arrive at the train station where you are loaded into cattle cars by armed guards. The doors close and you can see the faces of your family striped by the sunlight entering through the slats on the side of the rail car. Finally, you have had enough and you speak to your mother. "Where are we going?"

"Someplace they can watch us," she whispers.

"Why?" you ask.

"Because our country is at war, and we are Japanese."

"But, grandma came here when she was a girl. We are Americans!"

"We have no choice. The government says we must go." She turns away in silence, ending the conversation.

The year is 1942 and you are one of more than 100,000 people of Japanese ancestry, more than half of which are American citizens, who have been forcibly removed from their homes and moved to internment camps. This was the result of Executive Order 9066 signed by President Franklin D. Roosevelt on February 19, 1942, which authorized the Secretary of War to establish "military areas" from which any and all persons may be excluded. The order was given in an effort to keep those loyal to Japan from conducting espionage against the United States during wartime.

Discussion Questions

1. What were the facts relevant to the case?

2. What is the major question to be decided?

3. You be the judge: Was this order constitutional?

4. How do you think the Supreme Court ruled? Why?

Section 2: The Actual Case
Korematsu v. United States (1944)

Fred Korematsu was an American-born citizen of Japanese ancestry, born and raised in Oakland, CA. Unable to enlist in the military at the beginning of World War II due to poor health, Korematsu nevertheless aided in the war effort by helping to build ships. When Japanese Americans began being relocated to internment camps, Korematsu tried to pass himself off as a Mexican American so he could stay close to his girlfriend. His ruse was discovered, however, and he was arrested, convicted, and moved to the "military area" of San Leandro, CA (Street Law & The Supreme Court Historical Society, 2002a).

Fred Korematsu challenged his conviction, however, based on the fact that he was never suspected of any activity hindering the war effort. Instead, he reasoned that the internment was based solely on the race of the people being relocated. This, he claimed, made the executive order unconstitutional.

The Ruling

The United State Supreme Court disagreed with Korematsu, with Justice Hugo Black delivering the majority opinion. The court ruled that protection against espionage outweighed the rights of an individual. Even though laws compelling the exclusion of a group of people were considered "constitutionally suspect," this action was justified during a time of "emergency and peril" (*Korematsu v. U.S.* [1944]).

The Aftermath

Soon after the war's end, American leaders seemed to find error in their actions. Congress passed the American Japanese Claims Act in 1948, which paid limited claims to some of the Japanese Americans who reported devastating financial losses. In 1976, President Gerald Ford announced that the relocation program was wrong. In 1980, President Jimmy Carter established a commission to investigate the internment. The commission stated that the Supreme Court ruled in error. In 1988, President Ronald Reagan signed the Civil Liberties Act of 1988, which paid survivors $20,000 each. In 1992, President George H. W. Bush increased the amount and issued a formal apology from the U.S. government (Street Law & The Supreme Court Historical Society, 2002b).

Korematsu challenged his conviction again, 40 years later. This time the U.S. District Court overturned his conviction, taking into account newly uncovered evidence. The U.S. Supreme Court, however, has not overturned its ruling of 1944, thus the original law (Executive Order 9066) remains constitutional (Street Law & The Supreme Court Historical Society, 2002b).

Making It Current

Does the U.S. government still treat groups of people differently based upon their race or ethnic heritage? How does this differ from the internment of Japanese Americans during World War II?

CASE 9:
THE SEGREGATED SCHOOL

BROWN V. BOARD OF EDUCATION OF TOPEKA (1954)

FOR THE TEACHER

Quick Reference

The Issue: The case challenged state laws requiring separate school facilities for Black students.

The Players:
Linda Brown—Student who was forced to attend a Blacks-only school. The case bore her name, as the petitioner, but she really represented many other similar petitioners from other states.
Thurgood Marshall—NAACP attorney, representing Brown, who argued the case before the Supreme Court.
Earl Warren—Chief Justice of the Supreme Court. Wrote the unanimous decision that "separate is inherently unequal."

The Ruling: Court ruled in favor of Brown, outlawing school segregation. Overturned *Plessy v. Ferguson* (1896).

Significance: Put a legal end to segregation in the United States, although it would take many years to actually abolish the practice.

Background

    Brown v. Board of Education (1954) is important for several reasons. First and most obviously, this decision overturned the doctrine of "separate but equal," established in *Plessy v. Ferguson* (1894), with the resounding statement that "separate is inherently unequal." This sounded the death knell for legal racial segregation. Unfortunately, although the case called for the end of segregation, answering the call with actual integration required decades of judicial action, legislation, and community activism.

This case also is important because it firmly established the Warren Court (the Supreme Court presided over by Chief Justice Earl Warren) as perhaps the most activist court in U.S. history. The Warren Court churned out one landmark case after another that sought to secure the rights of the individual against a powerful government. Ironic is the fact that Earl Warren, the former Republican Governor of California, was appointed by fellow Republican President Dwight D. Eisenhower. Many conservatives at the time regarded the Warren Court as unnecessarily activist, even overstepping the role of the Supreme Court. Eisenhower himself would have sought much slower, less wrenching solutions than those put into place by his own appointed Chief Justice.

SECTION 1:
THE SEGREGATED SCHOOL

Harold Wagner had been the principal of Miller Junior High School for 16 years and was not a man to be trifled with. In his youth, he played linebacker for the University of Nebraska, and followed up on this experience with a successful coaching career in Kansas before becoming a school administrator. On this occasion, however, he sat for the entire conference with a big artificial grin plastered across his broad face. The occasion was a meeting requested by Doris Johnson, a mother of four who was, in Wagner's opinion, a fearsome troublemaker. She also was Black.

The conversation went like this:

Johnson: I would like to take a tour of your school, Mr. Wagner.

Wagner: Well, thank you so much, Mrs. Johnson. We have a fine school with modern classrooms, plumbing, and a new auditorium. I understand why you would want to find out more about it. If you will just speak to my secretary out front I'm sure we could get you some literature.

Johnson: I don't want literature, Mr. Wagner, I'd like a tour.

Wagner: Oh, I'm sorry, I misunderstood. I'm sure we could arrange a tour for you this evening. Why don't you speak to my secretary out front—

Johnson: Mr. Wagner, I'd like to take a tour now.

Wagner: Ma'am, if you don't mind me asking, what is the purpose of the tour?

Johnson: I want to see if I want to enroll my daughter here. She's 12.

Wagner (mopping his brow): Oh. I'm afraid that won't be possible, Mrs. Johnson.

Johnson: The tour?

Wagner: No ma'am, not the tour. I think you know what I mean. Your daughter can't go to this school.

Johnson: And why not? Her grades are excellent.

Wagner: Oh, I'm sure they are. But, you know how it is.

Johnson: Just how is it, Mr. Wagner?

Wagner (sighs): She's Black.

Johnson: I know that. So, where is she supposed to attend school?

Wagner: There's another junior high across town. Washington. I'm sure you've heard of it.

Johnson: She's not going to Washington! Have you seen that place?

Wagner (crosses his arms and leans back): But ma'am, she has to. She can't go to school here, it's against the rules.

Johnson: Whose rules? I have a third grader who attends Crow Elementary right down the road. He's got White kids and Black kids in his class. Is this your rule Mr. Wagner?

Wagner: It's school board policy. Our elementary students go to school together, but in secondary we have separate schools for Negroes and Whites. There's less fighting this way. I'm sure you understand. Your daughter will be much more comfortable at Washington. Why are you doing this, Mrs. Johnson? It's been this way for as long as these schools have been here.

Johnson: That doesn't make it right. (Pause) You're really not letting her enroll?

Wagner: No ma'am. I can't allow that.

Johnson: Thank you for your time.

She politely got up and left. Three days later, Harold Wagner received a notice from an attorney that Doris Johnson was filing suit against him and the school district for violating her daughter's rights protected by the Fourteenth Amendment to the U.S. Constitution.

Discussion Questions

1. What do you think will be the result of the lawsuit? Explain your answer.

2. Does it make a difference in this case that some schools were segregated and some were not?

3. What legal basis was the school district using to have segregated schools (Hint: See *Plessy v. Ferguson*)?

4. What does the Fourteenth Amendment state about the issue in this case?

Supreme Court Decisions © Prufrock Press • This page may be photocopied or reproduced with permission for classroom use

SECTION 2: THE ACTUAL CASE
BROWN v. BOARD OF EDUCATION
OF TOPEKA (1954)

Linda Brown was a young Black student in the Topeka, KS, school system. She was forced by school board policy to attend an all-Black school that was farther from her house than the all-White school. When she tried to gain admittance into the all-White school, her request was denied by the school board.

The law, which allowed larger school districts to have segregated schools, was based on the 1896 Supreme Court ruling in *Plessy v. Ferguson*. In *Plessy*, the court ruled that states could require separate facilities for Blacks and Whites as long as the facilities were equal. This is known as the doctrine of "separate but equal," and was the basis for segregated public facilities up through the mid-20th century (Bradley, 1999).

Brown, with the help of the National Association for the Advancement of Colored People (NAACP), a civil rights organization, filed suit against the Topeka school board arguing that segregated schools violated the Fourteenth Amendment. Within this amendment it is stated that states must provide equal protection under the law, also known as the Equal Protection Clause. Brown's case was argued by Thurgood Marshall, who later became a Supreme Court justice (Bradley, 1999).

THE RULING

Although the district court agreed that segregation had a negative impact on Black students, it upheld the allowance of segregated schools based on the "separate but equal" precedent set by *Plessy v. Ferguson*. When the U.S. Supreme Court heard the case, however, it took the entire notion of separate but equal to task. The court was headed by new Chief Justice Earl Warren, a former Republican Governor of California. In the *Brown* case (which was combined with other similar cases from across the country), the court relied heavily on the now-famous doll study conducted by sociologist Kenneth B. Clark.

Dr. Clark's research included two groups, one consisting of White children and the other Black children. Each group was given Black dolls and White dolls to play with. When asked which dolls were pretty or good, children of both races chose the White dolls. But, when asked to pick the bad dolls, the children chose the Black dolls (Library of Congress, 2004).

The Supreme Court used this research to assert that segregating students on the basis of race negatively damages minority students to a point from which they can never recover. In a straightforward rebuke of *Plessy v. Ferguson*, the Court declared that "separate educational facilities are inherently unequal," and thus struck down the legal practice of public school segregation (*Brown v. Board of Education*, 1954).

The Aftermath

Unfortunately, the practice of segregation was not easily overcome. Even though the U.S. Supreme Court overturned the practice of legal segregation, getting the schools to integrate was a much more difficult task. In fact, it took a second Supreme Court case—*Brown v. Board of Education* (1955)—to order states to integrate schools with "all deliberate speed." But, even with the order of the judicial branch of the U.S. government, desegregating remained a difficult process. Many citizens, particularly in the South, were solidly against the idea of desegregation, and they worked actively to prevent it.

In addition to active prevention of desegregation, many tough obstacles remained in place to stop the process. Many cities had whole neighborhoods and school districts that were either all Black or all White. How were they to desegregate the schools that were the result of racial geography? This problem prevented some school districts from integrating for another 15 years.

Eventually, students of one race were transported daily, by school bus, across town to attend schools for the other race. This forced integration, known as bussing, was a controversial remedy to the segregation problem that continued into the 1990s, almost 40 years after *Brown v. Board of Education of Topeka*.

Making It Current

The Americans with Disabilities Act (1990) required businesses, schools, government offices, and the like to make their facilities more accessible to people with disabilities. In what ways is this similar to the intent of *Brown v. Board of Education* (1954)? How is it different?

CASE 10:
THE SEARCH

MAPP V. OHIO (1961)

FOR THE TEACHER

Quick Reference

The Issue: Can a state use improperly obtained evidence to convict a person of a crime?

The Players:
Dollree Mapp—Convicted of possession of obscene materials. Police searched her house, without her consent or warrant, looking for a dangerous fugitive. They discovered obscene materials, and she was subsequently convicted. She argued that the evidence was obtained in violation of the Fourth Amendment.

The Ruling: The Court overturned her conviction on the basis that the evidence was discovered during an illegal search.

Significance: Expanded the Exclusionary Rule, which placed strict rules on the gathering of evidence that can be used to convict someone of a crime. The ruling also incorporated the Fourth Amendment to the states.

Background

    Mapp v. Ohio is another of the long list of landmark cases decided by the Warren Court. In its ruling, the Supreme Court established precedents expanding the Exclusionary Rule (placing strict guidelines on how evidence in a criminal investigation may be obtained) and in tying the states to this new standard through the incorporation doctrine (see *Gitlow v. New York*).

The Court received tremendous criticism because, the critics argued, it would make law enforcement officers follow much tougher guidelines when conducting investigations. Critics argued that criminals would go free because of clerical or superficial errors made by police. Supporters, on the other hand, argued that *Mapp* set in place protections that should have been followed all along.

SECTION 1:
THE SEARCH

You are a policeman in Houston, TX. At 1:15 a.m., you receive a radio call from your dispatcher that an arson suspect is being harbored in a house in your area of responsibility—your beat. As soon as you respond to the dispatcher, however, the voice of another officer, Dale Seaver, crackles over the radio and informs dispatch that he'll meet you at the address for assistance. Because you work your area without a partner, you welcome the help of Officer Seaver, who has many more years of experience on the force. Within a few minutes, several other officers also have responded to the call. In this case, this particular arsonist is wanted for setting a fire in an industrial district that killed two firefighters.

You pull up in front of the house and it isn't a moment before Dale Seaver's car appears down the street. Soon the houses in the neighborhood are illuminated in the eerie and urgent strobe of six police flashers as you and the other officers surround the house. You and Seaver decide to take the front door. Before you can even decide what you're going to say, Seaver pounds on the door loudly with his fist. "Police!" he announces. "Open the door!"

Surprisingly, almost immediately, the small, scratchy voice of an elderly woman calls from the other side of the door. "What do you want?"

Seaver smiles and looks at you. "Do you think she was waiting on us?" You shrug.

"Ma'am, this is the police, we need to come in there. There is a dangerous situation and we need to come in."

"Do you have a warrant?" the old lady screeches back like a bird of prey.

Seaver chuckles this time, shaking his head. "Yes ma'am, we've got it right here."

You frown at Seaver. He has no warrant and you wonder what he's up to. He catches the hint and whispers, "This is a dangerous situation and we need to get in that house. What if he's holding her hostage? This could be our only chance to get her out of there safely and catch this killer at the same time."

Then, without warning, the door cracks open and the old lady sticks out her hand. "Let me see the warrant," she demands.

Seaver grabs the woman by the wrist and abruptly pulls her out onto the front porch and pushes the door all the way open with his foot as he lurches inside the darkened house. All the while, the woman is screaming at you to show her the search warrant. Before you know it, lights are going on in the house as the other policemen enter and begin to search for the arsonist. You feel like you have lost control of the situation and decide to go into the house to find out what Seaver is doing. The old lady follows you in and you go from room to room looking for Seaver.

You can hear doors opening and slamming as police search rooms and closets for the arsonist, but the search has turned up nothing so far. Finally, you go into the back bedroom and find Seaver standing over a small trunk at the foot of an unmade bed.

"What's in here?" he asks the old woman.

"Nothing!" she yells, getting more and more excited. "You never showed me a warrant, so you can't search that!"

Seaver bends down and unhooks the clasp and pops open the trunk lid. The old woman tries to close the lid, but you hold her back. Seaver looks up smiling. The trunk is almost full to the top with one-gallon zipper bags containing white powder. Field tests reveal that the substance is cocaine and the old woman is placed under arrest.

Discussion Questions

1. What problems or conflicts do you find in this scenario?

2. Does Seaver's rationale that this is a dangerous situation alter the need for a search warrant?

3. If you were the police officer in charge, would you do anything differently? If so, what? If not, why?

4. You be the judge: Was this a lawful search? Was this a lawful arrest? Why or why not?

THE ACTUAL CASE: *MAPP v. OHIO* (1961)

In May 1957, police in Cleveland, OH, received information that a fugitive bombing suspect was being harbored in the home of Dollree Mapp. When police arrived on the scene and announced their desire to enter the house, Mrs. Mapp refused to let them enter and then called her attorney. Finally, after opening the door, Mapp demanded to see a search warrant. One of the policemen waved a piece of paper claiming that it was the warrant and she quickly snatched it from him and stuffed it down the front of her shirt. Mapp was handcuffed and police started to search the house (*Mapp v. Ohio*, 1961).

The police searched all of the rooms, including the bedrooms and basement. When searching the basement, police discovered a chest containing "lewd and lascivious" photos and books. The police arrested Dollree Mapp for violating Ohio's law against possessing obscene materials. Mapp was found guilty in state court and sentenced to a women's reformatory. The police never turned over to court officials the so-called warrant that Mapp had snatched from the police officer (*Mapp v. Ohio*, 1961).

Mapp's attorneys appealed the conviction based on the argument that there was no warrant giving authority to search the house, making the search illegal. Therefore, the evidence obtained in the search—the obscene materials—could not be used in court. The Ohio Supreme Court ruled that although this argument was reasonable, the evidence could still be used in court because it was obtained in a harmless search of an object and not Mapp's body. Thus, they upheld Mapp's conviction (*Mapp v. Ohio*, 1961).

THE RULING

Next, Mapp appealed to the U.S. Supreme Court, which ruled that both the Fourth and Fourteenth Amendments applied to this case. The Fourth Amendment guarantees an individual's protection from unreasonable searches and seizures from the federal government. The Fourteenth Amendment

required states to also follow the Fourth Amendment. (See *Gitlow v. New York* and the incorporation doctrine for more information.) Therefore, the Supreme Court ruled that the evidence used to convict Mapp was obtained in an illegal search and that it could not be used against her in court, overturning the conviction (*Mapp v. Ohio*, 1961).

THE AFTERMATH

Mapp v. Ohio greatly expanded the Exclusionary Rule (the rule that requires that evidence be properly obtained to be used against a defendant). In fact, some critics argued that criminals would run free just because of technical mistakes made by police. However, as Justice Tom C. Clark wrote in his majority opinion, ". . . it is the law that sets him [the criminal] free" and that "Nothing can destroy a government more quickly than its failure to observe its own laws. . . ." (*Mapp v. Ohio*, 1961).

Mapp v. Ohio is representative of the Court's unprecedented movement to protect individual liberties during the 1950s and 1960s under the leadership of Chief Justice Earl Warren.

MAKING IT CURRENT

With the spread of global terrorism, do you think that governments should do whatever it takes to protect its citizens from terrorist attack, even if it means infringing upon the rights of individuals? Why or why not?

Case 11:
The Indigent Defendant

Gideon v. Wainwright (1963)

For the Teacher

Quick Reference

The Issue: Should states provide representation for defendants in criminal proceedings, as guaranteed by the U.S. Constitution?

The Players:
Clarence Gideon—Impoverished, and virtually illiterate, he was not given an attorney to represent him in a state trial. He was convicted, but later wrote his own petition to the Supreme Court.
Hugo Black—Supreme Court justice writing the majority opinion.

The Ruling: The court ruled that states must provide representation to criminal defendants and ordered a new trial for Clarence Gideon.

Significance: Incorporated the Sixth Amendment to the states.

Background

Gideon v. Wainwright is important because it represents one more element of the Bill of Rights that the Court incorporated to the states (see *Gitlow v. New York*). Here, the Court ruled that the right to counsel is so basic that its protection is guaranteed by the Fourteenth Amendment. But, the case also is instructive to the procedures of the court system and how one can petition the court for assistance. For example, Clarence Gideon, acting as his own attorney, filed a petition *in forma pauperis* (meaning that he was impoverished and could not afford to pay filing fees). This is a good case to use as a review of how cases can make it to the Supreme Court.

Finally, *Gideon* makes for compelling storytelling. Consider the fact that Gideon was almost illiterate, was charged with a crime he did not commit, represented himself poorly at trial, and then was convicted. While in prison he became a student of the law, filed and argued his own appeals, and then continued the fight all the way to the Supreme Court. Although Gideon is no role model for personal behavior, his story certainly is remarkable and serves as an inspirational backdrop upon which various lessons can be taught.

The fictional vignette, "The Indigent Defendant," includes an example of a petition for writ of certiorari requesting that the Supreme Court hear a case. It is written from the perspective of an indigent inmate much like Clarence Gideon.

SECTION 1:
THE INDIGENT DEFENDANT

Julian Franks rubbed his eyes before opening another envelope. He had been clerking for an associate justice of the United States Supreme Court for 2 years. Deep down he knew that he helped make history and he loved his job and the law. One aspect of his job, though, reading petitions, was not as exciting as he would have imagined. Supreme Court clerks read thousands of petitions for writs of certiorari every year and pass them to the justices for approval. Each petition is a request for the court to rule on a case being appealed by defendants from state supreme courts and federal district courts. Only about 150 of those thousands of requests are actually granted.

This request, however, caught his eye. First, the return address showed that it was mailed from a Mississippi state penitentiary. Second, the petition was handwritten in pencil, and in a scratchy printing style that revealed the writer's lack of formal schooling. But, most interesting of all was the simple accuracy of logic. As he read, he understood once again the importance of his work.

IN THE SUPREME COURT OF THE UNITED STATES OCTOBER TERM, 1961

David W. White, Petitioner
vs.
H. M. Phillips, Director, Division of Corrections.
State of Mississippi, Respondent

"Answer to respondent's response to petition for Writ of Certiorari."

Petitioner, David Wilson White received a copy of the response of the respondent in the mail dated sixth day of April 1962.

Petitioner is not an attorney so does not know the law like the respondent. But according to the rules of the court, the respondent has run out of time to respond. He had thirty days and that has passed.

The respondent says that a man can get a fair trial without a lawyer. I was put to trial and the State of Mississippi would not provide a lawyer for me after I had asked for one. I am poor and could not afford to get a lawyer.

I did not get a fair trial because I was not given counsel when I asked. I could not represent myself

---

fairly because I do not know the law of the courtroom like an attorney does.

    The respondent says that the Constitution of the United States does not apply to the State of Mississippi.

    Petitioner thinks that the Fourteenth Amendment protects citizens even if they are poor.

    Petitioner will attempt to show this Court that a citizen of the State of Mississippi cannot get a just and fair trial without the aid of counsel.

    Petitioner claims that the crime charged, burglary, never happened. He called the Federal Bureau of Investigation at the time and was told that they could not help.

    Petitioner asks that the Court disregard the response of the respondent because it was given past the due date set by the court.

Petitioner

Discussion Questions

1. What is the issue in this case?

2. Do you think the Supreme Court would have decided to hear the case based on the writ of certiorari above? Why or why not?

3. For what crime was Mr. White charged?

4. How could the State of Mississippi claim that the U.S. Constitution does not apply to the state? Does the Fourteenth Amendment apply in this case?

5. You be the judge: Do you think the Supreme Court upheld or overturned the defendant's conviction? Explain your response.

Section 2: The Actual Case
Gideon v. Wainwright (1963)

Clarence Earl Gideon was a poor drifter who was accused of breaking into a bar in Panama City, FL. However, the evidence linking him to this crime was somewhat weak. Because he could not afford an attorney to represent him at his trial, he asked the court to provide one for him as, he claimed, was guaranteed by the Sixth Amendment to the U.S. Constitution. The judge ordered that because his was not a crime of "special circumstance" (e.g., illiteracy, mental illness, youth, complexity of the charges) nor a capital crime, then Florida was not legally bound to provide Gideon with an attorney (Mikula & Mabunda, 1999).

Gideon was forced to represent himself at trial, and was incompetent in selecting and questioning his own witnesses and cross-examining the state's witnesses. He was sentenced to 5 years in state prison for breaking and entering and petty larceny. He believed that his Sixth Amendment right to counsel had been violated, so he began studying law books in the prison library. This research only strengthened his belief that he was wrongly convicted.

Gideon petitioned the State of Florida, through a writ of habeas corpus, to be set free due to his illegal imprisonment. This petition was turned down. Finally, he petitioned the U.S. Supreme Court for a writ of certiorari, in a handwritten document, asking that the court hear his case. The court allowed Gideon to file without paying the normal filing fees because of his indigent status (Mikula & Mabunda, 1999).

The Ruling

In *Betts v. Brady* (1942), the Supreme Court ruled that states must provide representation to defendants in capital cases (where the death penalty is offered) or in cases of special circumstances when the charges are complex or the defendant is illiterate. In his case, Gideon did not make a claim of special circumstances. The acceptance of Gideon's case meant that the Court would be reconsidering its previous ruling in *Betts v. Brady*. The question to be considered here was whether the right to counsel in a criminal trial, guaranteed in federal courts by the Sixth Amendment, is a right so fundamental that it falls under the protections offered in the Fourteenth Amendment (Mikula & Mabunda, 1999). That is, is it a right that should be incorporated to the states? (See the incorporation doctrine of *Gitlow v. New York*.)

Justice Hugo Black, delivering the majority opinion for the Court, wrote:

> From the very beginning, our state and national constitutions and laws have laid great emphasis on procedural and substantive safeguards designed to assure fair trials before impartial tribunals in which every defendant stands equal before the law. This noble ideal cannot be realized if the poor man charged with crime has to face his accusers without a lawyer to assist him.

Thus, the Court overturned Gideon's conviction and stated that its previous position taken in *Betts v. Brady* (1942) "was wrong" (*Gideon v. Wainwright*, 1963).

THE AFTERMATH

Gideon v. Wainwright (1962) is remarkable on several levels. On a personal level, Clarence Earl Gideon's persistence in studying the law and arguing his case is an inspirational story of the little man beating the odds. States would now be required to provide counsel to defendants who could not afford to hire their own. But, in the bigger picture, this case represents the expanded protections of the U.S. Constitution from abuse by the states. It also signifies the increased role of the Supreme Court in the protection of individual liberties.

MAKING IT CURRENT

Does the wealth of an accused criminal make a difference in the judicial process? What evidence have you seen to support your opinion?

Case 12:
The Confession

Miranda v. Arizona (1966)

For the Teacher

Quick Reference

The Issue: Do states have an obligation to not only protect a person from self-incrimination, but also to inform them of this right?

The Players:
Ernesto Miranda—As a police suspect, Miranda confessed to a crime without knowing that he did not have to do so or that he had the right to have an attorney present during questioning.
Earl Warren—Chief Justice of the Supreme Court.

The Ruling: The court overturned the conviction and established a guideline, known as the Miranda warning, to be followed by law enforcement officials when taking a suspect into custody.

Significance: It incorporated the Fifth Amendment (right against self-incrimination) to the states and set strict guidelines for law enforcement officials. It is considered one of many rulings the Warren court passed that greatly increased the rights of individuals.

Background

   Miranda v. Arizona is a landmark case that not only has changed police procedures in questioning suspects, but has been ingrained into the psyche of American culture, as well. Almost every adult knows that when one is placed under arrest, the suspect is warned that he or she has "the right to remain silent . . ." mostly because it is shown in countless television shows and movies.

Additionally, it is yet another ruling that uses the incorporation doctrine (see *Gitlow v. New York*) to tie another segment of the Bill of Rights to the states. In this instance, the Court ruled that the right against self-incrimination, guaranteed by the Fifth Amendment, was so basic that it was a right worthy of the protection of the Fourteenth Amendment.

To a great extent, this case also showed the irony of the Warren Court activism. Judicial conservatives were surely scratching their heads at the thought of Earl Warren, former prosecutor and Republican governor, presiding over a court that handed down an unprecedented number of rulings aimed at strengthening the rights of individuals, the accused, and minorities, often to the chagrin of the law enforcement community.

Suggested Activity Specific to *Miranda v. Arizona*

Have students conduct research on the following cases and then answer and discuss the questions that follow.

- *New York v. Quarles* (1984)
- *Oregon v. Elstad* (1985)
- *Illinois v. Perkins* (1990)

1. How do the cases listed alter the precedent set in *Miranda v. Arizona*?

2. Do you think the Court has expanded the rights of the accused or has it swung back in the other direction? Explain.

3. Do you disagree with the rulings in any of the cases listed? Explain.

SECTION 1:
THE CONFESSION

Zhi "Martin" Ching walked quickly, but quietly, through the deserted Dallas warehouse district. It was 2:30 a.m. and there was not a person in sight. He had slung over his shoulder a navy blue pillow case he used to carry the radio he'd just stolen from a car foolishly parked near a dark alley on Industrial Drive. He stopped for a moment to light a cigarette, fumbling to remove one of the black gloves so that he could get the cigarette out of the pack.

He was blowing smoke and steamy breath into the night air when he heard the squeaking of car tires taking a fast corner on the next block. Instinctively he dropped the bag behind a Dumpster and briskly walked away from the sound of the speeding car. He turned into a darkened alley where he would stay until the car passed and until the hair, now standing on the back of his neck, went back down. To his surprise and dismay, a Dallas police car screeched to a stop, blocking his exit from the alley. He turned in fear to escape but found that the other end of the alley was blocked by police, as well. He offered no resistance when the officers handcuffed him and placed him in the back of the car.

Martin refused to answer the questions of the police, but they didn't know whether he was just being difficult or if he truly didn't understand English. They discovered from his identification that he had only been in the U.S. for a month, and that he was a resident alien from the People's Republic of China. When they spoke to him, they did so in loud voices exaggerating the pronunciation of words.

"Mr. Ching, what were you doing in this part of town at this time of night?" The first officer shouted. Martin did not respond, but merely looked at the officer with a quizzical expression on his face.

"Mr. Ching, tell us where you have been this evening." No response.

"Mr. Ching, where did you put the radio you stole?" Still no response.

The officers, however, were undeterred by Martin Ching's silence. They knew that the police would send a Chinese interpreter in the morning, so there was nothing left to do but to continue to question. They reasoned that if a man was in a dangerous part of town in the middle of the night, then he probably knew enough English to get himself around town.

The questioning went on for 3 hours with no breaks. Martin Ching was tired, thirsty, and hungry, and he had to use the bathroom, yet their questioning continued. Finally, when he could take the pressure no longer he spoke up. "I need bathroom."

The officers looked at each other and laughed out loud. "Three hours you've been putting us on? No bathroom until you answer one question: Why would you risk getting deported over a car radio?"

Martin sighed. He could stand it no longer. "I only here a month and already lost job," he explained. "I need the money to eat."

Based on his confession, Martin Ching was convicted of burglary of a motor vehicle and placed in jail.

Discussion Questions

1. Do you think Martin was aware of his rights guaranteed by the U.S. Constitution?

2. Are city police bound by protections guaranteed by the *federal* constitution? Why or why not? (Hint: Review the Incorporation Doctrine from *Gitlow v. New York*.)

3. Do the police have an obligation to make sure that suspects are aware of their rights?

4. Do you think the police in this situation followed established procedures?

5. You be the judge: Would Martin Ching's conviction be upheld or overturned if this case was appealed? Why or why not?

SECTION 2: THE ACTUAL CASE
MIRANDA V. ARIZONA (1966)

In March 1963, police in Phoenix, AZ, arrested Ernesto Miranda for the rape and kidnapping of an 18-year-old girl. Miranda was taken into custody after his vehicle was described by the victim's brother. He was identified by the victim in a police lineup, and questioned by police for 2 hours. He finally confessed, having no knowledge of his constitutional rights against self-incrimination or his rights to have an attorney present. Later, when police showed him the victim he said, "That's the girl" (Gribben, n.d.).

In the trial, prosecutors relied on Miranda's confession to secure his conviction. Miranda's attorney objected to his confession being used as evidence against him because he had no knowledge of his rights that protected him from making a coerced confession. His objection, however, was overruled. He was sentenced to 20 to 30 years in prison for rape and kidnapping (Jacobs, 1999).

Miranda appealed the decision to the Arizona Supreme Court, but the conviction was upheld. Finally, Miranda filed for a writ of certiorari with the U.S. Supreme Court, which agreed to hear his case.

THE RULING

The Court was divided on the issue, offering a 5–4 ruling on the matter. Chief Justice Earl Warren (himself a former prosecutor) delivered the majority opinion. Warren reasoned that the right against self-incrimination (guaranteed by the Fifth Amendment) is basic to the validity of our judicial system. Therefore, before any custodial interrogation (i.e., when a person is being questioned about a crime after he or she has been taken into custody by police), a suspect must be apprised of his or her rights.

It must be explained to suspects in this situation that they have the right to remain silent, that anything said can be used against them, that they have the right to an attorney, or if they cannot afford an attorney that one will be provided, and that they may stop at any point in the questioning to assert these rights. Furthermore, the Court ruled, the right against self-incrimination is a right so basic that its protection must be provided by the states as guaranteed by the Fourteenth Amendment (*Miranda v. Arizona*, 1966). This being the case, the Court ruled that Miranda's conviction was based upon a confession illegally obtained. His conviction was overturned.

THE AFTERMATH

Critics of the Warren Court claimed that the rights of the accused were so strictly protected that police agencies would have trouble securing convictions against criminals. Civil libertarians hailed it as another ruling that strengthened the protections of individual rights. Whatever the opinion, however, the law enforcement community remains bound by the rules established by this case. Suspects are mirandized (read the Miranda warning off a card carried by most police officers) at the time of their arrest. The refrain of "You have the right to remain silent . . ." is known by most citizens who watch police dramas on television and in movies, and is a direct result of *Miranda v. Arizona*.

MAKING IT CURRENT

If the police come to your home and question you about an incident in which you were involved, must they read you your rights before the interview? Why or why not?

Case 13:
The Silent Protest

Tinker v. Des Moines (1969)

For the Teacher

Quick Reference

The Issue: To what extent can schools limit student speech, and is the wearing of symbols protected by the First Amendment?

The Players:
John and Mary Beth Tinker—Students who were suspended from school for wearing black armbands in protest of the Vietnam War. Filed suit against the district on the basis that the First Amendment (right to free speech) protected their right to wear the armbands as political protest.
Abe Fortas—Wrote the majority opinion for the Court.

The Ruling: The Court found in favor of the students, ruling that wearing armbands was a form of expression that is protected by the First Amendment. Also, it ruled that schools cannot restrict speech unless it substantially disrupts discipline at the school.

Significance: It expanded the protection of the First Amendment to include symbolic speech and set clear guidelines for school officials for protecting students' First Amendment rights.

Background

In *Tinker v. Des Moines*, the Court once again set out to clarify the protections of the First Amendment. In this case, the question posed is whether symbolic speech (the wearing of a black armband) is protected by the

Constitution: The answer is a resounding "yes." Additionally, the Court had to answer the question of whether speech can be restricted in public schools: The answer was a qualified "no." The Court, in an effort to clarify the conditions under which speech could be restricted in school, created the "Tinker test." Speech could be restricted, the court reasoned, when that speech would be reasonably be expected to "materially and substantially interfere with the requirements of appropriate discipline in the operation of the school" (Mikula & Mabunda, 1999).

Tinker v. Des Moines should be an interesting study for students, considering it is relevant to their own situations and desires. A study of *Tinker* will be surprising to students who think that free speech has no limits, and also to those who think that they have no guaranteed freedoms in school.

Suggested Activity Specific to Tinker v. Des Moines

Conduct research on the case *Texas v. Johnson* (1989) and answer the questions below.

1. Is flag burning considered protected speech?

2. Do you think there should be a constitutional amendment protecting the flag? Why or why not?

3. How does *Texas v. Johnson* differ from *Tinker v. Des Moines*?

SECTION 1:
THE SILENT PROTEST

When news came that Danny Wilson had been killed, that's when I decided I'd had enough. I was only 14, but Danny was my older brother's best friend since the third grade. I knew him well and there was no explanation for the war in Vietnam that could possibly justify Danny's death. As far as I was concerned, President Johnson had murdered Danny without actually having pulled the trigger; and Danny was just one of thousands. It was then that I finally understood what the protests were all about.

The next day, I was sitting in my high school cafeteria when I had an idea about a protest. I figured that any sort of march or "sit-in" would get me expelled from school, so I tried to come up with a more peaceful way of making a statement against the war. Finally, I remembered how my grandmother wore black when she was mourning my grandfather after he died. I decided that I'd wear a black T-shirt in protest of the war. One of my friends thought that the black T-shirt wasn't a bold enough statement. "How about if we paint a big red X on the front?" I said. "Then we would represent the thousands of lives that had been crossed out." My friend nodded in approval.

So many of my friends liked the idea that word quickly spread among the student body that we would all wear the black T-shirt on the following Monday as a silent protest to the Vietnam war. In fact, word spread so rapidly that it wasn't long before our principal, Mr. Weatherby, heard of the plan. On the Friday before our Monday protest, he made an announcement over the school public address system. "Any wearing of black T-shirts with or without insignia," he said, "will be considered a school disruption. School administration must oversee the orderly process of education. Bearing this in mind, violators of the T-shirt policy will be expelled from school."

That weekend I talked it over with my father. He understood my position against the Vietnam War, although he thought our idea about the T-shirt with the red X was melodramatic. He was not happy, however, that I was planning to violate the school's ban on these shirts. I explained to him that the shirt was to be a silent protest and that there was no way it could be disruptive. I told him that I couldn't imagine that they'd really expel us for a silent protest. I looked at it as freedom of speech. Isn't that what Danny was fighting for in the first place?

That Monday I wore the shirt against my father's wishes. As soon as I got to school, Mr. Weatherby called me into his office to tell me that I was expelled. I could return, he said, when I agreed not to wear the shirt. Surprisingly, when I came home, my father had a change of heart. A couple of weeks later, he sued the school district and I went to school without my black T-shirt. I had graduated already, but 3 years later our case was still in court—the United States Supreme Court.

Discussion Questions

1. Do you think a school's administration has the right to regulate how students dress other than what is specifically stated in the dress code policy? Why or why not?

2. Do you believe, as the student does in this case, that this is a matter of free speech? Explain your answer.

3. How far should school administration go in protecting the school against disruption?

4. How far should a student be able to go when exercising his or her right to free speech?

5. You be the judge: Who was right in the case above, the student or the administration? On what grounds do you base your answer? (Consider a review of *Schenck v. U.S.* [1919].)

Section 2: The Actual Case
Tinker v. Des Moines Independent Community School District (1969)

In 1965, John and Mary Beth Tinker were students in the Des Moines, IA, school system. They and some other students decided to wear black armbands to school as a silent protest to the country's involvement in the Vietnam War. The armbands were to be worn for a specific number of days, at the end of which the protesters would discontinue wearing the armbands and the protest would be over. When administrators in the district learned of the protest, they quickly adopted a new policy designed to stop the demonstration and any disruption to school that would occur because of it (*Tinker v. Des Moines*, 1969).

School administrators announced that they had established a new policy banning the wearing of black armbands. Furthermore, students who came to school with black armbands would be asked to remove them immediately. Any students who refused to remove the armbands would be suspended from school until they agreed to remove them. Among the students who decided to defy the order where John and Mary Beth Tinker. When the Tinkers arrived at school, they were asked to remove the armbands, and they refused. They were suspended from school and told that they could return when they had removed their armbands. The Tinkers finally returned to school, without armbands, on the planned end date of the protest and were allowed back into school.

The parents of the children, however, filed suit in federal court to stop the school district from enforcing the armband policy. The court agreed that the children were exercising free speech, but sided with school district officials who said that the ban was intended to avoid disruptions that might have been caused by the protest. The Tinkers appealed the case to the Federal Court of Appeals but were halted due to a tie vote by the panel. Finally, they appealed their case to the Supreme Court (Mikula & Mabunda, 1999).

The Ruling

Justice Abe Fortas wrote the majority opinion for the Court. In its proceedings, the Court had to decide whether wearing the armbands constituted "symbolic speech" and the extent to which this speech was protected by the First Amendment. Additionally, the Court had to decide whether schools have a higher authority to limit such speech. "It can hardly be argued," Fortas wrote, "that either students or teachers shed their constitutional rights to freedom of speech or expression at the schoolhouse gate" (*Tinker v. Des Moines*, 1969).

Fortas also reasoned that in order for schools to limit speech, they must show that the result of the speech would "materially and substantially interfere with the requirements of appropriate discipline in the operation of the school. . . ." Des Moines school officials failed to show any evidence that the armbands would have caused such a disruption (*Tinker v. Des Moines*, 1969).

Finally, the court found that Des Moines school officials did not prohibit all controversial symbols, but only the specific symbol protesting the Vietnam War—the black armband. This specific prohibition in effect supported one opinion over another. As Fortas wrote, "Clearly, the prohibition of expression of one particular opinion, at least without evidence that it is necessary to avoid material and substantial interference with schoolwork or discipline, is not constitutionally permissible." Thus, the Court ruled in favor of Tinker and struck down the school's rule against the black armband as unconstitutional (*Tinker v. Des Moines*, 1969).

AFTERMATH

Tinker v. Des Moines (1969) served to clarify further the question of what constitutes speech and which of these forms of speech are protected by the First Amendment. The threshold of when speech loses its constitutional protection in school (when it materially and substantially interferes with the operation of the school) has been called the "Tinker test," and has been used by the courts to clarify First Amendment cases relating to schools. This ruling was noteworthy not only because it helped to clarify the protections of the First Amendment, but also because it asserted the rights of students, which have not always been recognized. This ruling helps to set a standard of what is disruptive in school settings, and it sets that threshold rather high. In *Tinker v. Des Moines*, the Court once again wrestled with a recurring theme: balancing the concepts of individual freedom vs. collective security.

MAKING IT CURRENT

Why is a school dress code not considered a violation of a student's First Amendment right to express him- or herself? How could a dress code be written or enforced that would constitute a violation of the First Amendment?

CASE 14: THE SCHOOL SEARCH

NEW JERSEY v. T.L.O. (1985)

FOR THE TEACHER

Quick Reference

The Issue: Does the Fourth Amendment guarantee of freedom from unreasonable searches and seizures extend to school children?

The Players:
T.L.O.—Unnamed student who was expelled from school for possession of illegal drugs. School administrators searched her belongings based on a suspicion that she was in possession of cigarettes. She filed suit on the basis that school officials did not have probable cause to continue the search after the cigarettes were found.

The Ruling: The Court ruled in favor of the school district, stating that the student's Fourth Amendment right was not infringed upon because the search was based upon a "reasonable suspicion" that she possessed an illegal drug.

Significance: Although the Court affirmed that students are still protected by the Fourth Amendment in a school setting, it set a lower threshold for school officials to conduct a search than the threshold police must observe. Whereas police are required to have probable cause to search a suspect, school officials need only a "reasonable suspicion."

Background

New Jersey v. T.L.O. is another case that many students will find interesting. Often, students (and their parents) do not understand that, although students' rights are protected at school, the rules of evidence are not as strict for school officials as they are for the police. The Supreme Court established in *T.L.O.* that police need *probable cause* to conduct a legal search, whereas schools only need to meet the threshold of *reasonable suspicion*. That is, in order for a school official to conduct a search of a student or his or her property, that official must have a reasonable suspicion that the student is in possession of illegal items or items that violate school rules.

This ruling, which relaxed the evidentiary standard (at least for school officials), is also representative of the Rehnquist Court, which had the reputation for slowing the expansion of civil liberties that marked the last half of the 20th century.

SECTION 1:
THE SCHOOL SEARCH

Sarah Neville was a 17-year-old senior at Churchill High School. She was proud of her new car (which was really a hand-me-down Ford Taurus that had been driven by her older sister.) This was her first day to drive it to school and she couldn't stop talking about it to her brother Josh who was riding next to her on their way home. She pulled up to a stoplight and glanced over at Josh, a 14-year-old freshman, and saw that he was sulking.

"What? You're jealous? You can't even be happy for me for one day?" she asked.

"It's not about the car, Sarah. I got in trouble today," he said, looking out the window.

"You're always in trouble, Josh," she scolded. "Why was today any different?"

"The police came."

Sarah pulled quickly into a grocery store parking lot and turned off the engine and then gave Josh her full attention.

"What did you do?" she demanded. Josh sat silently looking out the side window. "Josh, look at me. What did you do?"

Josh refused to look at Sarah, but answered, "I got caught with cigarettes."

"You're 14 years old! You know better than that! And, what are you doing smoking in the first place?"

"I didn't even smoke them, Sarah, I swear!" Josh answered.

"Don't you even remember going to Grandma's funeral last year? Is that how you want to go? She didn't even look like herself at the end! Is that what you want to be?"

"I didn't smoke. Blaine gave me his pack of cigarettes in the bathroom during third period and we were going to smoke them there but we changed our minds."

"That's so stupid. So, how did you get caught?"

"Mr. Clayton called me in during fourth period and searched me."

"He searched you? How did he know that you had cigarettes?"

"I don't know. He said a staff member told him that it looked like something was exchanged between Blaine and me."

"Did you see a teacher in the bathroom?"

"Well, Mr. Tolar came in right after Blaine gave me the cigarettes, but I don't think he saw them. We were pretty surprised when he came in."

"Are you sure that's it? That doesn't sound right to me, Josh. Mr. Clayton said that someone said you had 'exchanged' something?"

"Yeah, that's all he said. Then he told me to empty my pockets onto his desk, and the pack was in my pocket."

"He didn't say that someone saw you with cigarettes?"

"No, Sarah, I told you what he said."

"You could've been exchanging anything, Josh. A candy bar, or a pencil."

"So what, Sarah? He searched me and he found them. The police gave me a ticket, and I have to go to court." Josh said.

"I don't think he had probable cause to search you, Josh." Sarah said softly.

"What do you mean?"

"We learned about it in civics. In order to search you, they have to have probable cause. He didn't have any idea you had cigarettes; I think he was just searching to see what he'd find," she explained. "I don't see how this can hold up in court."

"Maybe Mom won't be as mad," Josh said hopefully.

Sarah replied, "No, that was really stupid and Mom's still going to kill you, but maybe the judge won't."

Discussion Questions

1. What are the facts that are important to this case?

2. Why do you think Mr. Clayton searched Josh?

3. Is Mr. Clayton bound by the same rules regarding searches as the police?

4. Can authorities search whomever they want at any time? Why or why not?

5. You be the judge: Did Mr. Clayton conduct a legal search? Explain your answer.

SECTION 2: THE ACTUAL CASE
NEW JERSEY v. T.L.O. (1985)

T.L.O. was a student at a New Jersey high school in 1980. (Because she was a minor, her initials were used to protect her identity.) She was caught smoking in the bathroom with another friend. Although her friend admitted to smoking, T.L.O. claimed that she had not. Faced with T.L.O.'s denial, the assistant principal decided to conduct a search of her belongings. In conducting the search, the assistant prin-

cipal found cigarettes, and when he removed them from her purse, he also found papers used in rolling marijuana cigarettes. Having a new suspicion that T.L.O. might be in possession of drugs, the assistant principal continued the search and found marijuana, as well as information indicating that T.L.O. was dealing drugs. He immediately called T.L.O.'s mother and the police. Later, she admitted to selling marijuana at school and she was charged with delinquency (Street Law & The Supreme Court Historical Society, 2002c).

T.L.O. fought the charges, however, claiming that the evidence used to charge her was obtained by an illegal search. T.L.O. was convicted by juvenile court and the conviction was upheld on appeal. T.L.O. had tried to argue that her Fourth Amendment right had been violated. The courts ruled that because the assistant principal found evidence of marijuana use while search-ing for the cigarettes, he was acting with the "reasonable suspicion" that, according to the courts, is all that is required by a school official. The New Jersey Supreme Court thought otherwise and overturned T.L.O.'s conviction. The state of New Jersey, then, appealed this decision to the U.S. Supreme Court (Street Law & The Supreme Court Historical Society, 2002c).

THE RULING

The first question that the Court had to settle was whether school offi-cials are bound by the Constitution at all when conducting searches, and it ruled that school officials are bound by the Fourth Amendment. However, according to the majority of the Court, school officials are only bound to the strict wording of the Fourth Amendment, which prohibits unreasonable searches and seizures. That is, searches must be based on a reasonable suspicion that a search will turn up evidence that a crime has been committed. As the Court's majority opinion states, "Such a search will be permissible in its scope when the measures adopted are reasonably related to the objectives of the search and not excessively intrusive in light of the age and sex of the student and the nature of the infraction." Thus, T.L.O.'s conviction was upheld (*New Jersey v. T.L.O.*, 1985).

The Aftermath

Although the Court affirmed that students have protections guaranteed them in the Constitution, it also affirmed a looser set of rules for school administrators regarding searches. School officials can search students without warrants and without probable cause (as is required of the police) and are held only to the easier standard of "reasonable suspicion." In the wide scope of rulings from the second half of the 20th century, *New Jersey v. T.L.O.* (1985) is an example of the Supreme Court setting limits on the individual liberties it had been broadening for decades.

Making It Current

Why do school officials have a lower threshold to meet than police concerning when they are allowed to search a student? Does your school's published code of conduct explain its policy of searching students? What are your thoughts about the policy?

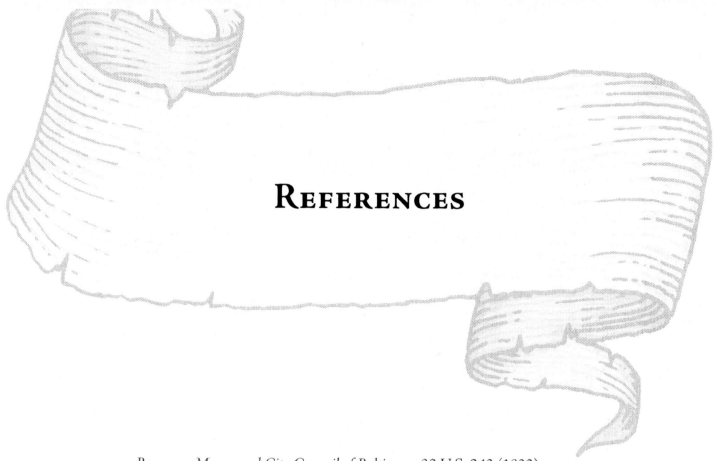

REFERENCES

Barron v. Mayor and City Council of Baltimore, 32 U.S. 243 (1833)

Betts v. Brady, 316 U.S. 455 (1942)

Bradley, M. R. (1999). Brown v. Board of Education. In Salem Press (Eds.), *U.S. court cases: Volume 1: Law and the courts* (pp. 154–160). Pasadena, CA: Salem Press.

Brandenburg v. Ohio, 395 U.S. 444 (1969)

Brown v. Board of Education of Topeka, 347 U.S. 483 (1954)

Brown v. Board of Education, 349 U.S. 294 (1955)

Dred Scott v. Sandford, 60 U.S. (19 How.) 393 (1856)

Edwards, G. C., III, Wattenberg, M. P., & Lineberry, R. L. (2002). *Government in America: People, politics, and policy* (10th ed.). New York: Addison-Wesley.

Ex Parte Milligan, 71 U.S. 2 (1866)

Gibbons v. Ogden, 22 U.S. 1 (1824)

Gideon v. Wainwright, 372 U.S. 335 (1963)

Gitlow v. New York, 268 U.S. 652 (1925)

Gribben, M. (n.d.). *Miranda vs. Arizona: The crime that changed American justice*. Retrieved July 10, 2007, from http://www.crimelibrary.com/notorious_murders/not_guilty/miranda/3.html

Hamdan v. Rumsfeld, 126 S. Ct. 2749 (2006)

History Place. (1996). *The Dred Scott decision*. Retrieved September 14, 2007, from http://www.historyplace.com/lincoln/dred.htm

Jacobs, R. (1999). Miranda v. Arizona. In Salem Press (Eds.), *U.S. court cases: Volume 2: Law and the courts* (pp. 355–360). Pasadena, CA: Salem Press.

Korematsu v. U.S., 323 U.S. 214 (1944)

Library of Congress. (2004). *"With an even hand": Brown v. Board at fifty.* Retrieved September 14, 2007, from http://www.loc.gov/exhibits/brown/brown-brown.html

Mapp v. Ohio, 367 U.S. 643 (1961)

McCulloch v. Maryland, 17 U.S. 316 (1819)

Mikula, M., & Mabunda, L. M. (Eds.). (1999). *Great American court cases: Volume 1: Individual liberties.* Farmington Hills, MI: The Gale Group.

Miranda v. Arizona, 384 U.S. 436 (1966)

Mount, S. (2001). *Constitutional topic: Martial law.* Retrieved September 14, 2007, from http://www.usconstitution.net/consttop_mlaw.html

New Jersey v. T.L.O., 469 U.S. 325 (1985)

PBS Online. (1998). *Dred Scott's fight for freedom.* Retrieved September 14, 2007, from http://www.pbs.org/wgbh/aia/part4/4p2932.html

Plessy v. Ferguson, 163 U.S. 537 (1896)

Sanson, J. P. (1999). Plessy v. Ferguson. In Salem Press (Eds.), *U.S. court cases: Volume 2: Law and the courts* (pp. 404–406). Pasadena, CA: Salem Press.

Schenck v. U.S., 249 U.S. 47 (1919)

Street Law, & The Supreme Court Historical Society. (2002a). *Korematsu v. United States: Background summary and questions.* Retrieved September 14, 2007, from http://www.landmarkcases.org/korematsu/background3.html

Street Law, & The Supreme Court Historical Society. (2002b). *Korematsu v. United States: Did the court err in Korematsu?* Retrieved September 14, 2007, from http://www.landmarkcases.org/korematsu/didthecourt.html

Street Law, & The Supreme Court Historical Society. (2002c). *New Jersey v. T.L.O. (1985): Background summary and questions.* Retrieved September 14, 2007, from http://www.landmarkcases.org/newjersey/background3.html

Swann v. Charlotte-Mecklenburg, 402 U.S. 1 (1971)

Sweatt v. Painter, 316 U.S. 455 (1942)

Tinker v. Des Moines, 393 U.S. 503 (1969)

ABOUT THE AUTHOR

Jeffrey Stocks' teaching experience includes 7 years of teaching Advanced Placement and gifted and talented classes in U.S. History, U.S. Government, and macroeconomics in the Katy Independent School District in Katy, TX. He was a charter member of Katy ISD's Pre-AP/AP Social Studies Vertical Team and helped write the district's curriculum in macroeconomics. He graduated with a bachelor's degree in English from The University of Texas at Austin and earned a master's degree in curriculum and instruction from the University of Houston. He is currently a high school administrator in Katy ISD.